To Pat and Don,
To our wonderful and loyal Friends

Love,
Bob

School Desegregation

A Shattered Dream?

Robert W. Peebles, Ph.D.

VANTAGE PRESS
New York

Cover design by Susan Thomas

FIRST EDITION

All rights reserved, including the right of
reproduction in whole or in part in any form.

Copyright © 2007 by Robert W. Peebles

Published by Vantage Press, Inc.
419 Park Ave. South, New York, NY 10016

Manufactured in the United States of America
ISBN: 978-0-533-15729-7

Library of Congress Catalog Card No.: 2007921014

0 9 8 7 6 5 4 3 2 1

To my grandchildren

Contents

Acknowledgments	vii
Prologue	1

Part I Pittsburgh

Richard Wallace	15
Dale Frederick	21
Moe Coleman	26
Stanley Lowe	33
Helen Faison	41
Al Fondy	46

Part II Boston

Tracy Amalfitano	53
Ruth Batson	56
Carolyn Chang	59
Muriel Cohen	63
Judge W. Arthur Garrity, Jr.	68
Charles Glenn	73
Frank Jones	77
Jean McGuire	81
Bill Ohrenberger	86
Gary Orfield	89
Paul Parks	94
Tom Payzant	99
Bob Peterkin	104
Bob Sperber	111
Robert (Bud) Spillane	117

Sam Turner	121
Marty Walsh	126
Bob Watson	130
Kevin White	133
Charles Willie	137

Part III Louisville

Lucien Gates, III	145
Rev. Louis Coleman	146
Claudia Runge	146
Carmen Weathers	148
Beverly Moore	148
Robert Douglas	150
Joseph H. McMillan	151

Part IV Alexandria

Tim Elliott	155
Bill Euille	166
Christine Howard	176
Mark Howard	180
Gilbert Mays	190
Melvin Miller	196
Mickey Moore	201
John Porter	207
Roy Smith	214

Epilogue	223

Acknowledgments

My appreciation goes to all these interviewees who so generously gave me more than ample time to explore issues and to pose questions requiring careful thought. Indeed, some of the questions were not only provocative but sometimes audacious. Some interviews were more revealing, divulging keen insights that proved particularly valuable.

My sons, Jim and Scott, and my stepsons, Scott and Jon Burr, all experienced racial incidents in and out of schools. My stepson Scott Burr read and critiqued each page of the manuscript.

Freda Merriweather and Claude Purvis guided me through the schools and neighborhoods of Louisville.

A special note of gratitude goes to Dr. Robert Adeson, a retired surgeon and dear friend, who spent many hours reviewing my manuscript and asking the tough questions that required direct answers.

My deep appreciation goes to Jerry Murphy, then Dean of the Harvard Graduate School of Education, who made me a scholar with special privileges to use all that school's resources.

Jay Matthews of *The Washington Post* gave me valuable suggestions about how to proceed.

No one deserves appreciation more than Dorothy Mulligan, who arranged interviews, transcribed their comments from my handwritten notes, and edited the recollections of the interviewees. She then returned them to me for rewriting their comments into readable language.

The constant support and patience endured by my wife Elisabeth cannot be measured adequately. Her selfless sacrifice of time and her forbearance of my frequent absences, sometimes a matter of a week or longer, are examples.

School Desegregation

Prologue

For sixty-one years, segregation has affected my life, beginning as a young draftee in 1943 when I became a Seabee with the 28th Special Battalion. Growing up on Cape Cod in a quiet all-white neighborhood, I was largely unaware of the accepted discrimination that existed in my village, indeed in my state and in New England.

I joined the U.S. Navy in Boston along with twenty other recruits, many of whom were longshoremen. We boarded a train bound for the District of Columbia's Union Station and were transferred there to a train headed for Richmond and Williamsburg, Virginia, and Camp Perry for basic training. It was my first encounter with blatant racism. The railway stations had separate drinking fountains for whites and colored. Toilets were segregated, as was the entire state of Virginia, supported by law.

We were trained in a boot camp by seasoned marines who used racist terms regularly, referring to the slowest and least coordinated as "niggers." How well I remember that staff sergeant shouting at me, "You left your momma; I'm you f_____ mother now!"

When we landed on the island of Samar during the battle of Letye Gulf, I became seriously ill after sleeping in the mud during the monsoon season. I wound up in Fleet Hospital 114 with both lungs full of fluid. After three years in Veterans Administration hospitals, I was diagnosed with tuberculosis and had two thorocoplasty operations, during which the surgeons removed five ribs and totally collapsed one lung. During the procedure the surgeon told me, "We had to use some nigger blood, but don't worry, you'll be OK."

When my tuberculosis was in remission I attended Boston University's School of Business. During the summer I had a relapse, which led to the aforementioned operation. A year of complete bed rest provided me with plenty of time to read. There was no television in the sanatorium, so I listened to the radio and read many books, most on American history. The fascination with history convinced me that teaching history was my goal.

Upon recovery and with my tuberculosis in remission, I entered Boston University's School of Liberal Arts, graduating with a BA in 1952. I was accepted as a student in the Harvard Graduate School of Education, becoming a candidate for the Master of Arts in Teaching program. The program, run jointly by the College of Liberal Arts and the School of Education, combined courses in history and philosophy in the "yard" and only the necessary education courses to become certified.

Part of the MAT program included a half-year internship in which I gained my initial teaching experience working with outstanding teachers of history and English at Lexington High School, a few miles north of Boston. My graduation from Harvard in 1953 will always be remembered by the sonorous call to the stage by then-president James B. Conant: "Will the candidates for the degree of Master of Arts in Teaching please draw near."

Sidney P. Marland, then Superintendent of Schools in Darien, Connecticut, came to Cambridge and recruited me to teach history at Darien High School in 1953. He later moved to the same position in Winnetka, Illinois, and Pittsburgh, Pennsylvania. Eventually he became U.S. Commissioner of Education during Richard Nixon's administration. Some years later he hired me as an assistant to the superintendent in Pittsburgh.

During my years in Darien (1953–1965), I was accepted as a Ph.D. candidate at New York University. The 1954 Brown decision calling for school desegregation had a deep impact on me, and my students at Darien High School were thoroughly involved as we discussed the issue of race and arranged for student exchange visits with New York City schools.

Darien was a totally white Anglo-Saxon community. Indeed, it received national and negative publicity when the theaters began showing the Academy Award-winning film, *Gentleman's Agreement*, starring Gregory Peck. All of this provided me with motivation to become actively engaged in the school desegregation movement.

New York City was a short forty-mile commute from Darien, and from 1957 to 1967 (with the exception of two years) I worked on my doctorate. In 1960–61 I was a John Hay Fellow at the University of California, Berkeley, and in 1965–66 I took a sabbatical leave from Darien High School to complete my dissertation. By June 1966 I was more than ready for an urban education experience.

I became an assistant to Superintendent Marland in 1966. For two years I was immersed in what was considered an exciting innovative plan to desegregate the public schools in one bold citywide move. Marland immodestly called it "Pittsburgh's Magnificent Gamble."

What follows is an insider's view of four attempts to desegregate schools—each different, ranging from failure to varying degrees of success. The locations are Pittsburgh, Pennsylvania; Boston, Massachusetts; Louisville, Kentucky, and Alexandria, Virginia. I hope that my own experience plus insights gained from interviews with participants in each of these cities bring a clearer understanding and a wider perspective of the overwhelmingly complex issue of desegregation.

Pittsburgh

On the night of April 4, 1968, all hell broke loose in the Hill District of Pittsburgh. This neighborhood lit up in flames as storefront after storefront went down, windows crashed reminiscent of Kristalnacht in Nazi Germany. Black rage erupted as people learned of the assassination of Martin Luther King, Jr.

Passionate emotions were already growing intense in Pittsburgh's public schools. Initial enthusiasm in the earlier 1960s over the Great High Schools Plan had changed to sharp skepticism, ranging from the college university community to neighborhoods throughout the city. Black leaders led the attack, pointing out the overwhelming number of black children being bused compared to white students. Prior to the night of King's assassination, black and white students rioted at Oliver High School on the city's north side. Fights broke out. Stones were hurled while teenaged girls formed rings, shouting chants, cheering on their young warriors.

Few issues have affected Americans more than school desegregation. Emotions were fierce, pitting neighborhoods against each other as desegregation supporters battled against staunchly opposed segregationists during the 1960s. The struggles continued in the succeeding decades, but significant changes in attitudes and plans have developed.

Back in the 1960s and 1970s, the intensity of feelings expressed at school board meetings is hard to exaggerate. Fed by media coverage, the public focused on school desegregation. The fate of many politicians was determined by stands taken for or against desegregation.

Of all these school districts dealing with school segregation, perhaps Boston received the most media attention. Who can forget those front-page photos of helmeted, masked police marching down Boston streets in the mid-1970s, using night sticks to force back angry hordes of people from their own ethnic neighborhoods? One had to be there to feel the degree of hostility displayed at community and school board meetings. Politicians actively involved are still vividly remembered—Kevin White, Louise Day Hicks, Joseph Moakley, Raymond Flynn, and

Michael Dukakis—to name a few. School superintendents came in and out of Boston regularly during those years. The main issue, central to the superintendent's tenure, was desegregation.

Boston

Few know or remember that in 1954 Chief Justice Earl Warren cited Boston as a city that eliminated segregation in 1955 and was in compliance with the law (Roberts v. the City of Boston, 1955). Accounts of Boston's desegregation efforts have been written. Probably the most dramatic is the Pulitzer Prize-winning book, *Common Ground*, written by Anthony Lucas. Judge Arthur Garrity, the federal judge who was responsible for monitoring the Boston school desegregation plan, claims that Lucas was not accurate. "I believe he had his story already written in his head before he started to write," he said. "It's like a novel with deliberately drawn characters.

Boston, during those tragic years, had a five-member school committee (board). Four were Irish Americans immersed in rough-and-tumble city politics; the remaining person came from an old Boston Brahmin family (Lee), who was not only eccentric but lived in the past. In short, he was completely out of it while he puffed on his water pipe.

In contrast to Pittsburgh's elegant and formal board room, Boston's school committee room was ordinary, with the five committee members sitting on a raised platform facing rows of metal chairs for citizens who came to lobby them.

In the mid 1960s, the Boston chapter of the NAACP had a forceful and vocal education committee led by Ruth Batson, a well-known community activist. She later acquired much acclaim for running the respected and state-supported METCO program that buses inner-city black students to bordering and outlying suburbs of greater Boston. During Batson's tenure as chairman of the NAACP education committee, she staged a sit-in at a school committee meeting. She and her supporters refused to leave unless Boston desegregated its schools. The meeting closed, and the next day headlines in Boston papers threw more coal on the fires beginning to burn in the city—a few years later, literally!

Louisville

In Louisville, Kentucky, long-established Jim Crow laws were unconstitutional in 1960. This segregated school district moved ever so lethargically toward desegregation. While the 1954 Brown decision officially struck down the dual school system, the city managed to retain its segregated patterns.

Before the 1954 decision, the surrounding county (Jefferson County) was also legally segregated. Like Louisville city, the county also remained essentially segregated for several years following 1954. Not until 1975 with the merger of the city's schools with those of Jefferson County did the opportunity open to establish a county-wide desegregated district.

A variety of desegregation plans with their accompanying redistricting, attitudes and positions began to change. When I presented my evaluation of the latest plan to the Jefferson County School Board before a packed house on October 24, 1994, these changing views clashed.

The well-known and highly respected civil rights leader in Louisville during the 1960s, Lyman Johnson, rose to speak. Now elderly and physically handicapped, he scolded those in the audience who had opposed the current plan. The opponents were younger, angry, and articulate. Johnson told them, "Don't go back to the days of segregation. You may control your black neighborhood schools, but you will still be like small fish in a pond."

The response that night was a polite rejection of Johnson's position. Support for high quality neighborhood schools was strongly voiced. These African-American spokespersons were tired of seeing the neighborhood children bused to other areas of the county, even though these were successfully educating children.

Details of the changing desegregation plans will be shown in the Louisville section of the book.

Alexandria

Across the Potomac River, opposite Washington, D.C., lies the city of Alexandria. Over the years since George Washington roamed its streets, the city has become a vibrant cosmopolitan community of 130,000. No longer a port city with tobacco warehouses, the city is approaching gridlock within its 15 square miles. Ethnic groups from Central America, Asia and the Middle East mix with native African-Americans, white Virginians, and white professionals from all over the country.

Although the city's white population is now about 70 percent, the public school district's population is predominantly minority—45 percent African-American and 20 percent Hispanic and Asian. Obviously, a large number of white families send their children to private and parochial schools.

Before the 1960s, Alexandria had a dual school system and was part of Virginia's plan of massive resistance to desegregation. Even then, it was more a traditional southern city. Although the school district took a few reluctant steps to integrate its schools, it essentially delayed initial efforts to integrate "Negro" students.[1]

With the retirement of T. C. Williams as superintendent of schools in 1962 and the hiring of a new superintendent, John C. Albohm, in 1963, the Alexandria schools moved more swiftly to desegregate. The passage of the 1964 Civil Rights Act, which included significant aid to education, stimulated efforts to desegregate schools.

In the mid 1960s, the city's three high schools were merged into one large high school, ironically named T. C. Williams. One consequence of this high school merger was the undefeated football team of 1971 that won the state championship. This story has turned into the popular movie, *Remember the Titans*.

Initially, T. C. Williams High School was a two-year school for juniors and seniors with the former George Washington and Francis C. Hammond High Schools serving freshmen and sophomores. The all-black Parker-Gray High School was phased out in 1964.

The astonishing change in Alexandria between 1954 and 1965 is nearly incomprehensible to native Alexandrians. They remember a quiet southern city of 62,000 in 1954, one that was solidly segregated. By 1965 the city had become increasingly cosmopolitan, with a population of more than 100,000. The school district's resistance to the Supreme Court's 1954 desegregation decision was as adamant and disingenuous as its school board policies legally allowed—similar to the state's massive resistance policies.

These four cities have their own stories to tell about school desegregation. To hear the voices of individuals who experienced desegregation efforts brings alive the stress and turmoil of these years.

No scientific system was used to select the interviewees, and much depended upon the degree of involvement, positions held, and availability. The resulting cross section of people provides insight to a dramatic, even traumatic, slice of late 20th-century American history.

Note

1. *Dissertation of Mark Howard,* An Historical Study of the Alexandria, Virginia, City Public Schools, 1954–1973, 1976.

Part I
Pittsburgh

Pittsburgh today stands in sharp contrast to the "smoky city" image of pre- and immediate post-World War II years. Perceptions change slowly and there remain many people who still refer to the smoky city. Now it is a revitalized, attractive city with several green, spacious parks, outstanding hospitals, museums, a noted symphony, live theater and art galleries scattered throughout the city. The university community is vibrant, led by Carnegie Mellon and the University of Pittsburgh.

One only has to drive from its new international airport through the Fort Pitt tunnel to experience a spectacular view of the "Golden Triangle." The Monongahela and Allegheny Rivers flow into the Ohio River and the city reveals a remarkable confluence of three rivers surrounded by skyscrapers housing new industries like aluminum, steel, and banks.

Civic leaders, powerful CEOs, scholars, planners, architects, and philanthropists coined the changes as "Pittsburgh's Renaissance." Borrowing on this term, a similar team of leaders, this time including educators, began to refer to Pittsburgh's "second renaissance" during the early 1960s.

At that time, the city of Pittsburgh received nationwide attention with its plan to build five "great high schools" strategically located to desegregate its secondary school population in one grand stroke. Each school was to accommodate 5,000 students. The plan was called Marland's "magnificent gamble," referring to Sidney P. Marland, who became Pittsburgh's school superintendent in 1963. Marland brought together an impressive team of administrators, urban planners, architects, and educational consultants who developed the "great high schools" in theory, schematics, models, and slide shows taken around the country. The reality is that not one great high school was ever built.

Lessons may have been learned from this experience, but what was once hailed as an answer to the woes plaguing large city school systems came crashing down in the midst of economic costs along with political and community opposition.

In 1964, Pittsburgh, roughly comparable to Boston, had a dwindling population of about 600,000. Its student enrollment was approximately 75,000 with 37 percent constituting "Negro" students. The parochial schools then enrolled 46,000 pupils. Back then, the average age of Pittsburgh's high school buildings was fifty-three years, the newest opening forty years earlier. Like other older Northeastern industrial cities, the city had well established ethnic neighborhoods with traditional residential areas becoming high density ghettos for the poor, underprivileged and segregated black population.

How implausible it seems now when the mantra "smaller is better" is sung by school boards and education gurus across the nation. How cyclical ideas revolve around public school reform efforts! A look back at the literature on education in the late 1950s and 1960s reveals how popular was the large comprehensive high school. In 1959, James Conant, the noted chemist and former president of Harvard University, wrote in his book *The American High School Today:* "The enrollment of many American public high schools is too small to allow a diversified curriculum except at enormous expense."

He argued for a comprehensive high school sufficiently large to meet the needs of all of its students that included a required academic curriculum and an array of elective courses plus an extensive program of extracurricular activities. Indeed, it was at this time that the concept of an education park seized the attention of educators. This idea required sites sufficiently large to include a comprehensive high school with feeder elementary and junior high/middle schools in close geographic proximity.

As Pittsburgh and other urban districts investigated the possibility of education parks, the idea of the great high schools emerged. Forty or more acres were needed to establish these education centers. Each was designed to relate to the freeways and rapid transit routes that connected with shopping centers, housing developments, and cultural centers in a massive effort to revitalize the whole city. This was truly a remarkable and bold example of city officials, school administrators, and community leaders attempting to re-energize and desegregate a city school system. Now, thirty years later, the city's schools are largely minority and no great high school exists.

What follows are interviews with individuals who were involved with desegregation and race issues in Pittsburgh. They include former Pittsburgh school superintendents, an academic, a former student during those years, and teachers' union leaders then and now. Obviously, this is a limited sampling and many other interviews could be conducted. Yet the comments of these six people, given freely, and unedited, provide insight that helps explain the Pittsburgh story.

Richard Wallace

Richard Wallace, now a professor at the University of Pittsburgh, had a highly successful tenure as the superintendent of the city's public schools from 1980 to 1992. To serve for twelve years as a superintendent in a major city is no mean accomplishment. Pittsburgh, like many other urban school districts, confronted the challenges of school desegregation during these years, and in measurable ways, largely succeeded, not only with its desegregation plan, but also in raising the level of academic achievement of its students.

I found Wallace working at his computer in a small office in what is called the Quadrangle Building, a large modern complex of office buildings occupying the historic space of what formerly was Forbes Field, the long-time home of the Pittsburgh Pirates. For an hour, this soft-spoken, scholarly looking man recounted his experiences as superintendent in this industrial city.

"I had no experience in desegregation before coming to Pittsburgh. My home town was Harverhill, Massachusetts, a former textile mill town near the border of New Hampshire. This was a working class community, nearly all white. I grew up, went to college in Southern Maine, and received my master's and doctor's degrees from Boston College. I taught in Arlington, Massachusetts, became a high school principal in an upper middle class suburb of Boston, and eventually became a superintendent of schools in Fitchburg, Massachusetts.

"Coming to Pittsburgh in 1980 was quite a contrast to my previous assignments. And almost immediately I was faced with a crisis involving the courts and a failing desegregation plan.

For fifteen years, the (Pittsburgh) Board of Education had dragged its feet before coming up with a desegregation plan in 1980. It was my responsibility to implement this plan in a most contentious and distrusting atmosphere. If the Board had not taken action in the spring of 1980, the courts would have moved in and probably taken over the school district. They just barely beat the courts.

"We were under the jurisdiction of the state's Human Relations Commission, and for twelve years we had to report regularly to this arm of the state responsible for monitoring school desegregation. There was no federal takeover.

"When I arrived in Pittsburgh, there were about 47,000 students, and the racial makeup was roughly 50 percent black and 49 percent white. In Pittsburgh, there was no significant Latino or Asian population. And for the next twelve years we stayed very close to those percentages and numbers—perhaps by 1992, 52 percent black and 48 percent white. During this time we were able to attract a lot of white students back into the system.

"Basically, we developed a very extensive magnet school program and we marketed it very aggressively. It got to the point where we had parents camping outside certain schools for up to a week or two prior to the opening of schools because registration was based on a first-come, first-served system. We were getting a lot of publicity all over the country. This worked very effectively for us, and the magnet schools are still very strong in the city.

"I remember one time when the mayor came to my office wanting to get his kid into the Sterrett Classical Academy (an elementary school), and I said, 'Mr. Mayor, you just have to get in line with the others.' We were being watched by many citizens who were looking for just such examples of political favoritism. In the late 1980s we converted to a lottery system. In effect, we had to buy our way into that system by guaranteeing parents that if they had a child in a particular magnet school, they would send siblings to the same school.

"For the first four years (1980 to 1984), we were monitored closely by the state's Human Relations Commission, largely because of a suit brought against us by an opposition group. The court decided that what the Board of Education had done was all right, but not enough, and they directed us to work with the Human Relations Commission to further enhance the desegregation of the schools.

"Essentially, the Board decided not to bus elementary students across the rivers (Allegheny and Monongahela). If elementary schools were possible to be racially integrated within the geographic regions of the city they were, but no youngsters were bused across the rivers. At the middle school level, all of the schools were racially integrated by busing, and children were bused all over the city. So at the secondary school level, basically, we worked it out with the Human Relations Commission, explaining that if they tried to force us to do it with certain schools, it would racially unbalance all the other schools.

"For the first three or four years, I had to negotiate with the Human Relations Commission as we tried further to integrate the elementary schools and the high schools. And we did it again through magnet programs. I convinced them that if we were to create special programs, we were able to integrate schools voluntarily. For example, we made South High School a high quality vocational school, working closely with area businesses. At Schenley High School, which was 87 percent black, we established a teacher center in 1981. When we started there, it was the lowest achieving secondary school and it is now the second ranking school in the city. For ten years, it has been 50 percent racially balanced. We also established special schools in high-tech, international studies, and the International Baccalaureate Program.

"To support these magnet programs, we developed a feeder system enabling students to move from elementary through high school in schools they had chosen. Beyond the magnets, what was key to our success was the School Board, which became united.

"When I first came to Pittsburgh, the Board was split 5-to-4 on everything, and one of the first things I did was to conduct a needs assessment survey of the district and the entire city. We covered citizens who had no children, parents whose youngsters were not in the public schools, and, of course, public school parents. These data were presented to the Board in January following my arrival the previous September. They then voted the priorities they wanted me to work on that emerged from these data. This action brought the Board together on virtually everything, and for more than a decade we had unanimous vote on nearly every item that came before it for action.

"By 1986, the Board had changed significantly with only three members left from the Board that had hired me. So we did another needs assessment, and had the Board vote another set of priorities, which kept that Board together.

"Interestingly, the fellow who became Board president, an African-American and strong advocate for desegregation, had been a 'doubting Thomas' in the early 1980s. I remember how he testified before the Human Relations Commission and said our plan would not work. Three years later, when we went to testify again in Philadelphia, a fellow Board member reminded him of how he was opposed to our plan, including the magnet program at Schenley High School where his children went. Jake, now the Board president, replied: 'I was wrong. It *is* working!' He became the strongest supporter of the plan and rallied the black community behind it. In five years, the achievement of black children nearly doubled, over 60 percent of the national norms.

"We kept adding to our magnet programs and began working with parents to bring back to our public schools those students who had left for private schools. Parents held teas and coffees for these private school parents who attended meetings for the purpose of selling our schools and persuading them to return their children to the public schools.

"Of course we had things working for us; scores were going up, the magnet schools were attractive, integration was working, and there were no problems with our desegregation plan. And, ultimately, the state Human Relations Commission became very supportive. The mayor, who had been quite cool to our efforts, enrolled his children in our schools.

"What has happened in the last few years is a sort of unraveling of the segregation plan. For years, South Hill parents, largely white, resented sending their kids across the river (Monongahela) to the middle school in the Hill (African-American) district, and they pushed hard for a school of their own. Well, they finally got their neighborhood school about three years ago. This encouraged other parents anxious for their kids to go to school in their neighborhoods, and there has been an ebbing away from the unified arrangement that established a systemwide set of K–5, 6–8, and 9–12 schools. Now there are some schools that are K–8, and most likely other changes will occur.

"In looking back on those years (1980–1992), we were successful, but not at all free from tension. Over time, the black community generally became very supportive. There was a group in the Homewood-Brushton community (largely African-American) that resented my demotion of a black deputy superintendent. And they just never let up, even though this position was filled by a very competent black woman who did an outstanding job.

"When I first arrived in Pittsburgh in 1980, I was asked by a lot of people what I was going to do about desegregation, and I said, 'Nothing, since the case is in the courts, and until that's resolved, we are going to concentrate on the root problem, and that is unequal education. We are going to focus on improving student achievement of all students, irrespective of race or socio-economic status.' We had about nine months before the court decision came down, and by that time we really got up a head of steam. Within a year we had improved student achievement and that continued for the next five years.

"So the critics sort of backed off as well as the (Pennsylvania) Human Relations Commission, because they saw things improving, and the Board established as one of its priorities the improvement of the black segregated schools. We developed a school improvement plan designed to raise achievement in these schools. And we did! Our pride and joy was a school that was ranked 57th among 57 elementary schools and made it to the top ten within three years.

"In Phase Two of our school improvement plan, we trained principals and matched administrative interns for two years with principals of high-achieving black schools. Several of these interns became successful principals using techniques learned during their internships.

"The future of the city's schools depends upon leadership. If they hire an able superintendent and if the Board doesn't get into micro-managing, the schools should continue to do well. But I am concerned. The current Board is deep into micro-management and that's a problem. The new superintendent is leaving and his successor will be key.

"Finally, it is crucial to maintain the tremendous support we have had from the foundations, the business community, and the city itself. Obviously, the state will play a vital role with the amount of money it provides to support urban schools. More than thirty million dollars came from foundations like Mellon, Heinz, Ford, and the Allegheny Conference, and they began to realize returns on their investments."

June 7, 1999

Dale Frederick

The headquarters building for Pittsburgh Public Schools is classical in appearance—architecturally and functionally. For many years, Pittsburgh superintendents and school boards have occupied austere and impressive spaces, unchanged but beautifully maintained.

On June 8, 1999, the current superintendent, Dale Frederick, was in the middle of packing his personal belongings as he prepared to leave for another superintendent's position in Mesa, Arizona. He says it was a job he could not turn down because it was his hometown and the roots in him are still strong. A barely two-year stay in Pittsburgh was sufficient for him to gain an appreciation of the city and its schools.

"I grew up in Arizona and southern California, going to elementary schools in both states. I finished high school in Tucson, Arizona, and being a native American, I feel very much at home there.

"My first experience with desegregation was in Tucson where I became involved with school attendance areas, transfers, and boundaries. After becoming an assistant superintendent in Tucson, I went to Dayton, Ohio, and helped design a systemwide magnet school program for their secondary schools. Both Tucson and Dayton gave me valuable experience that helped to prepare me for Pittsburgh.

"In Pittsburgh, like many other cities, schools were built close to each other in minority neighborhoods. This inevitably played a major role in early efforts to desegregate schools. Since these schools were all black, the bodies were there, and initially, resistance was weak. So busing these kids seemed an easy part of early desegregation plans, which dealt primarily with numbers and percentages. Community participation was lacking and little thought was given to preparing families for the change. Making kids move to white neighborhoods did not necessarily improve their education. Just sitting next to someone of different color had little positive effect on test results.

"The beginning years of desegregation saw inadequate preparation for the children affected by these moves and for their parents. Quality programs designed specifically to enhance learning and diversity were absent. Dick Wallace (Pittsburgh superintendent from 1980–1992) had a good run, and during his twelve years the school district was relatively stable. The budget was supported well, both by the city and state, with much help coming from business and the foundations. The magnet schools have held up well and our numbers are still quite similar to enrollment and racial percentages that existed twenty years ago.

"But I am concerned about the city's future—the school district and the city. Our most serious problem is funding. There has been a downward spiral for the past five to ten years. When I came aboard, I had about four months to overcome a deficit of more than twenty million dollars. The biggest reason for this huge budget problem is the change in the financial formula for special education. Prior to 1991–92 the state covered about 60 percent of the costs for special education. Now the school district pays about 70 percent from its general fund budget. Naturally, this has been very tough for the school district, very significant! There has also been a decline in revenues to the city. Business revenue is down, population is declining in the city, and it's not a pretty picture.

"The school board is now divided, particularly over the issue of neighborhood schools. There are philosophical and political differences leading to a 5-to-4 split in votes on the board.

The majority of five consists of four whites and one African-American. The minority of four is two whites and two African-Americans. Interesting! I sense a trend moving toward neighborhood schools.

"Pittsburgh is a great city and its greatest strength and its greatest weakness are one and the same—its diversity. Pittsburgh is very cloistered in its communities. As a school district, we deal with 88 or 90 individual and distinct communities, and these enclaves make dealing with issues like diversity and desegregation really difficult. It's interesting that one of my board members refers to the neighborhood school issue as an ethnic cleansing process.

"Some of our magnet schools are absolutely superb! The traditional academy system is working. The International Baccalaureate and Technical Academies are working, as are the creative and performing arts magnets. The others work, depending on the schools. Opposition to our schools is growing and the most serious threats are financial, vouchers, and charter schools. Vouchers for private and parochial schools as well as the charter schools take significant money from our public schools. Governor Ridge supports vouchers and speculation is that he will succeed in having the state legislature approve his voucher plan. (In 1999, he was unsuccessful.)

"If the confidence of the community in the public schools is lost, if the school board fails to design a system that responds to the needs of the community, and if finances do not change in support for the schools, I see a very bleak future. I think there is a five-year window of opportunity for things to come together before the system implodes. And when that happens, it won't be just the schools. It will be the city as well.

"We (the schools and the city) have been working together on a common approach to legislative action that will support and focus on our needs. Prior to this cooperative approach, we were separate and did things our own way. Failing to recognize our mutual needs, we were adversaries with the city facing its own budget crises and tending to focus on the school district to keep the pressure off themselves. In this past year, we worked closely with the city council and went to Harrisburg together to lobby for legislation that focuses on Pittsburgh. This helped us and the city.

"There is a pattern here where many parents will send their children to elementary schools, take them out during the middle school years, and send them back to public high schools if they are successful in getting them into those options (magnets) they prefer. The reason for this is because the middle schools were where the most significant effort was made for desegregation. Our comprehensive, traditional middle schools were not looked upon as safe quality and disciplined places for education. However, if you look at our magnet middle schools, they are burgeoning. We don't have enough spaces to accommodate the demand. But if you look at our traditional, comprehensive middle schools, we have space galore. So what happens is parents circumvent the system and go to private or parochial schools if they can't get their kids into the magnet middle schools they like. In the last four to six years, there has been a move to some K–8 buildings.

"That's what is going on in Pittsburgh. Fortunately, we are still able to recruit teachers, and Pittsburgh is regarded as a good place to teach. We probably had 300 to 400 positions to fill this year and we had around 1200 applicants. The situation with administrators is different, since there is a tendency to look inside the system. We should begin to look beyond the city for capable administrators.

"Pittsburgh has been able to maintain a significant middle class population, both white and African-American. This provides a base of stability in our student population. And for the last ten years the city has maintained its enrollment. Fifty-six percent is now African-American, and the Latino population remains relatively insignificant.

"The city is very complex, very sophisticated. Yet there is a small-town feeling about it."

Moe Coleman

Few people know better the city of Pittsburgh than Moe Coleman. Born, bred, and trained in the city, he worked in the mayor's office during the civil rights movement of the late 1950s and 1960s. He was also a member of the Pittsburgh Board of Education when desegregation efforts were planned and implemented. Now he is near retirement and completing a career as a professor of urban planning at the University of Pittsburgh. His office on the 23rd floor of the famed Cathedral of Learning Building provides powerful vistas of the former smoky city.

Coleman's comments are deeply reflective and reveal his active participation in the emotional and exciting events of the 1960s, '70s, and '80s.

"I grew up in Pittsburgh and went through its public schools when they were essentially segregated by ethnic neighborhoods. My first job was working as a social worker in a settlement house in the Hill District, an all-black neighborhood. One of our leaders was John Brewer, who was the principal at Miller School. He later became the first African-American Assistant Superintendent of Schools.

"My first serious involvement with school desegregation came when the city tore down part of the Hill District to make room for the civic arena, one of the first facilities to have a retractable roof. Our initial objective was to desegregate school faculties. When I went to school, the first African-American teacher came in the late 1930s. At Alderice High School, where I went, there were zero African-American teachers.

"Pittsburgh was a segregated city, and yet, with all of its segregated parochialism, it was far ahead in social legislation.

Under mayors like David Lawrence and Joseph Barr, we had passed public-accommodation and fair-housing laws before state and national laws were passed. So we were always concerned about race issues, but not necessarily school desegregation. This issue came to the forefront in a dramatic way in the 1960s with the 'Great High Schools' Plan (see prologue). I must say, it took the city by storm and captured national attention. Although the idea was brilliant, these schools were never built—for a number of reasons. In hindsight, having high schools (there were to be five) housing 5000 kids sounds like a nightmare. But it occupied our attention for several years from the middle 1960s to the 1970s. Significant land was purchased in different areas of the city and much demolition was done in East Liberty. Perhaps most important was the raising of the issue of school desegregation to the top of the list of citywide goals.

"When I got on the school board, the state's Human Rights Commission issued an order to desegregate, which had the support of the board. Fellow board members Gladys McNairy (African-American), Chuck Cooper (the first African-American to play in the National Basketball Association), Bob Kibbie (who became Vice-President of Carnegie Mellon and later the President of the State University in New York), and I were all advocates for desegregation. There were many conflicting pressures, and a growing division in the African-American community over the issue. The old white liberal coalition with black leaders was weakening as more African-American nationalists gained popularity.

"One of the first things we had to decide was what to do with the Great High Schools Plan. We had already bought huge amounts of land and now faced the problem of explaining how to run these immense high schools. Our assistant superintendent for business was very worried about these complex financial systems and had been skeptical about them while serving as the city's comptroller back in the sixties. The Board was concerned about the heavy investment being placed on the high school level, and I don't think the State Commission on Human Rights would accept integration at the high school level alone. And there was the question of putting kids together in high school when they lacked any experience being together earlier—no relationships at all.

"The race riot we had at Oliver High School on the Northside in 1968 provided a vivid example of what could happen, especially in 5000-pupil high schools being planned. It was a frightening experience. White and black kids, out of class, throwing rocks at each other—girls lined up on the periphery like cheerleaders urging on young warriors. Police arrived and used mace to quell the rioting. I was there, and do you know what? The black student leader of the rioting, Stanley Lowe, now heads the Housing Authority for the city of Pittsburgh. Actually, we had a number of riots during those years. Stanley Lowe also ran the Manchester Redevelopment, which is one of the most interesting projects in the country because it uses historical preservation as a way to revitalize a neighborhood and make it beautiful. Isn't it interesting to see how a former radical student leader of thirty years ago becomes a city leader? It reminds me of Congressman John Lewis and so many others who became remarkable leaders out of the turmoil of earlier times of desegregation, the Vietnam War, and civil rights struggles.

"Since the time of the Great High Schools debate there has been a sharp decline in the city's population. From the 1960s when we had about 700,000 people in Pittsburgh, the city now has roughly 400,000. It may be plateauing, but we are not growing. Of course this affects the schools, and if the Great High Schools had been built, there would have been a lot of empty space in those schools.

"The one school that was built (Beshear) is large, but not as large as the planned Great High School. Actually, we closed the downtown Fifth Avenue High School and South Hills High

School. So we did build a large high school on land we had purchased, and the students of former Fifth Avenue and South Hills High Schools were integrated at the new Beshear High School on the south side of the city.

"Knowing that the Great High Schools Plan was doomed, we looked at what our options were. We had all this land and owed all this money. There was fear among school board members about doing too much extensive busing at the elementary level, so we came up with the idea of trying to tie neighborhoods together by connecting middle schools with elementary schools. This scheme required large-scale middle schools. We actually built two large middle schools, and my wife, the teacher, said 'You are insane!' And she was right. If you are going to have open classrooms and bring in kids from age twelve to fifteen, the most agitated, hormone-flowing group imaginable, you're asking for trouble. And this is not even considering racial differences. Well, you just know we had severe management problems.

"By the 1970s, even earlier, there was division among African-Americans with the older, integration-oriented NAACP and Urban League confronting a growing militant, younger African-American leadership calling for separate and equal schools. This latter group considered desegregation as patronizing.

"We began to put more money into low-income area schools. Let's face it, there was very little opportunity for African-American kids at that time in the Pittsburgh area. It was still a pretty segregated town. The combination of low expectations combined with lack of incentives for good jobs led to poor performance in school.

"Oh yes, there was a lot of tension in my life over racial integration. I remember being called in the middle of the night during my years on the board. Many of the calls were from my own neighborhood, because I was on the integrationist side. And we could never go to a party without getting beat up verbally.

When I was in the mayor's office in the 1960s, nothing compared to the emotions stirred up by the school board. It was *truly* intense! And this was at the height of the civil rights revolution. My wife and I had to go to this dying restaurant on the north side so I wouldn't be recognized. Hell, it was like a mafia movie where I would make sure the table and my back were against the wall. We finally moved to the north side, where we still live. Similar emotions, I'm sure, were displayed in other cities.

"For a major urban school system, I think Pittsburgh is doing quite well. We have many fewer students, and part of the reason is Pittsburgh has the second-largest population of people over sixty-five years of age. Add to this a traditionally large parochial school system, and you have significant reasons for a relatively small public school enrollment.

"After I left the school board, I became interested in the idea of the magnet school. It has worked well in other places, and it certainly has helped our school system. For example, Schenley High School had always been overwhelmingly an African-American school. It is now integrated, thanks to its International Studies Program that became so attractive. This magnet school's achievement scores have risen dramatically.

"A major change in how school boards are elected has caused problems. Not only are members no longer appointed—they are now elected by districts rather than at large. This ensures politicking by board members anxious to provide patronage and other favors for their constituents. It also leads to the board moving from policy-making to administrative matters. And I'm afraid this is happening now. There is also more tension between ethnic groups, especially whites and blacks. How completely different from the days when the board considered the superintendent as its chief executive officer!

"We must recognize that school desegregation was one aspect of a much broader civil rights movement. Clearly, there have been significant gains. The African-American population has seen its middle class grow enormously. And its opportunities have grown similarly. Think back to when we were in school, and none of us would believe that the elite schools in the country would be turning out very highly qualified African-American graduates. At this level, upward mobility for working-class and middle class African-Americans has been extraordinary, even within a racist climate. Obviously, a lot of racism remains.

"The question we have not been able to deal with effectively is how to reach the inner city kids. We have created a two-tiered social system in the African-American community. While opportunities have opened for many, the poor and unskilled black population finds itself with less opportunity in a city with vastly fewer manufacturing jobs. And the mills (steel) have left the city. The economic change taking place today is comparable to the changes that occurred in the 19th century that led to the Industrial Revolution. It's hard to imagine how vast a change is happening. Today's Lexus automobile has more computer energy than what was required to send a man to the moon. The power of the microchip is unimaginable. To think that when the new millennium comes, the whole society would be crippled and unable to function if the computers don't work—that the whole society would come to a halt—is inconceivable.

"We have to figure out how to produce the technical ability of young people who are out of the technology and bring them into it. How do we begin to deliver into low-income neighborhoods, urban and rural, the ability to compete in an economy that is changing radically? The schools have a special responsibility to do this.

"If we do not produce that learning ability, we are going to have a two-tiered system of inequality more powerful than what we've had before. Yes, I think the tensions at the bottom of the ladder are dangerous and could become even revolutionary.

"Maybe school desegregation hastened suburbanization in the country. But the GI Bill, the ability to get cheap housing, the interstate highway, all played a role. Running away from racial tension was a factor, but not the only one. In looking back, I think I and others were denigrating to the white working class. We called them 'rednecks,' but they were trying to hang onto their limited resources. You can understand why they disliked intellectuals commenting on issues affecting their families. Sure, there were racists among these ethnic groups."

August 25, 1999

Stanley Lowe

Stanley Lowe is the executive director of the City of Pittsburgh's Housing Authority. Now approaching fifty, he shows the leadership qualities displayed as a student at Oliver High School on the north side of the city in 1968. His spacious, well-appointed office, with photos of civil rights heroes, reflects his own involvement and energy. Malcom X's portrait overlooks his desk. From this ninth-floor office one can sense Pittsburgh's history with a view of a dynamic downtown, the Monongahela River, and rail lines. Engraved plaques in the lobby of this beautifully restored building indicate that it was built originally for the Jones Laughlin Steel Company in the late 19th century. Then the only blacks allowed in the building were janitors.

Lowe is a tall, solidly built man who speaks directly, leaving little room for ambiguity. Much has happened to him since high school days. He has been an active participant in the changes affecting Pittsburgh over the past thirty years.

"Other than some of the stuff we did in high school, I haven't played a major role in desegregating schools. I have played a role in being concerned about African-Americans and their relationship to the educational process. I have been more of a spectator since leaving high school.

"Oliver High School was a very painful period in my life. I grew up in Manchester on the north side of Pittsburgh. Manchester in those days was 85 to 90 percent white and did not become an African-American neighborhood until 1968 or 1969, after the assassination of Martin Luther King, Jr.

"It is a story of white flight, similar to other stories of white flight during that time across the country. I remember asking my mother and being very shocked to learn that there are more white people in the world than black people.

"I remember it being a difficult situation at Oliver High School. Oliver did not prepare black students; that wasn't its role. Today it would be OK to ask questions from an African-American point of view. Back then it was not OK. I remember once sitting in class and I loved history. And the teacher said Benjamin Franklin's son was not admitted to William and Mary College. I had done some reading and knew that along with Harvard and Yale, William and Mary was one of the oldest schools in this country. I remember saying to the teacher, 'Excuse me, did you say Benjamin Franklin's son was not admitted to William and Mary College?' She said, 'Yes.' I asked why. She explained that she could not tell me why. And I said, 'Oh no, no, you've got to tell me. Ben Franklin, one of the signers of the Declaration of Independence, Ambassador to France, inventor of the pot-bellied stove. *His* son wasn't admitted? No, no, you've got to tell me why.'

"She again said she couldn't. After class she apologized for bringing it up. I continued to insist that she tell us. Well, this led to a confrontation with the whole class looking on. I said, 'You're going to tell us, because if you don't, I'm going to make a nuisance of myself, and you are going to send me to the principal's office. He will ask me why I am in his office. And I will tell him you wouldn't tell us why Benjamin Franklin's son wasn't admitted to William and Mary College. So why don't you just short-circuit this routine and tell us right now?' She said she would tell us if I would agree to drop the subject. She went on to explain how teachers have to follow lesson plans and that she will be reviewed in her evaluation. She then said that this son was born out of wedlock and that this was unacceptable in those days. I said, 'Oh, he was a bastard!' She pointed out that we agreed to drop the subject.

"My point in telling this story is that this was an example of selective history. To this teacher and to Oliver High School generally, what may have been relevant to African-American students did not matter. We were irrelevant. There were some good teachers at this school, but that's not the point.

"In the late 1960s, the black students were 20 percent of the enrollment. History was being taught to us the way it was thought it ought to be taught. And it wasn't just history. It didn't matter what may have been relevant for us. We were just there.

"During these years the Vietnam War and civil rights actions were happening. The Bidwell Church and Reverend Jimmy Joe Robinson had contact with a priest I came to admire greatly. This was Father James Groppi and Bidwell arranged a bus trip for young people to Milwaukee to meet Groppi. We watched this priest in action. He was leading marches for integrated housing every night. I got to know him very well. We used to go on these long marches through white neighborhoods chanting, 'We're not going to let Mayor Myer turn us around, turn us around.' The youth movement of the NAACP was there selling T-shirts and sweatshirts that had printing on them quite different from, let's say, Welcome to Penn State or the usual rah-rah stuff. I bought a couple of them. One was a gold sweatshirt that had white lettering saying 'Black Is Beautiful, Baby.'

"I remember wearing this sweatshirt to school one day, not thinking anything about it. The principal stopped in the hallway and said to me, 'Take that shirt off. You can't wear that here.' I said, 'What are you talking about?' He said, 'That shirt saying Black Is Beautiful, Baby.' I said, 'What!' And he said, 'That's insubordination! You're suspended.' I responded, 'Do you see that shirt over there that says Penn State? What is the difference?' All this led to a major upset in the school cafeteria. I think he overreacted, but you must recall the high intensity of emotions at that time. This episode spilled over and led ultimately to the race riot we mentioned earlier. I probably overreacted also. Before it was over, I got arrested. Black Americans were becoming more aware of who they were at that time—more conscious of their heritage.

"I remember once saying in Spanish class, 'Why don't you teach us Swahili?' There was no such thing as black college tours. We didn't know anything about such colleges. Had it not been for Dr. Norman Johnson, I would not be here now. He stepped into my life when there were no African-American mentors.

"Norman Johnson came to Oliver High School after seeing the story of the riot on TV. He was then teaching at Carnegie Mellon University and wanted to know if there was anything he could do. He asked me what were my plans for college. I told him I wasn't going to college because I wasn't college material. And do you know what he did? He picked up the phone and called the college president of Shaw University—just like that! Johnson came to know some of us through the riots at the school and following Martin Luther King's assassination. He became my mentor, came to my house and talked with my mother about the need for me to go to college. I explained to him that my high school graduating class had 225 kids and my ranking was 212. Plus the trouble I'd been in makes me a very unlikely candidate. Yet he insisted, and this was the first time in my life I saw an African-American demonstrate power. I saw him pick up a phone and talk directly to a college president of a black college and say to him that he has a student that has potential, and wanted him admitted. He asked what day he could send me. I had never seen anything like that in my life.

"At that time Norman was also working for Community Action Pittsburgh under Dave Epperson, now Dean of Social Work at the University of Pittsburgh. They flew me down to

Charlotte. You will never know what it's like for an African-American male to leave his home environment and go to an African-American college and be accepted for you who are and at the level you are at. And then, on top of that, to be introduced to African-American geniuses you had never before seen in your life.

"In my first two weeks there, they sent me to this lecture series. We had to go. I remembering seeing this old lady standing on the stage talking about being a sharecropper. It was Fannie Mae Hammer, and she told us how she worked on desegregation in Mississippi. Here I was, eighteen years old, hearing this old lady receive seventeen standing ovations. It blew me away. The president of the college was so overwhelmed by all this interaction he made her an adjunct professor.

"Now put yourself back in Oliver High School at that time, when there was absolutely no connection with what was going on in black colleges. As African-American kids in a majority white high school, we were just there, largely ignored, and certainly not understood. We were in an environment where we constantly had to struggle.

"Today we talk about diversity as if it were a normal matter, an OK thing. Back then, there was no such thing as diversity. My father was a Pullman porter for forty years. To him, A. Philip Randolph was a genius, a great guy. I and my buddies fell in love with Stokely Carmichael and H. Rapp Brown because the world was so vastly different. We were struggling over what to do with Martin Luther King.

"For me it was a time of confusion, it really was." (At this point in the interview, Lowe's voice is softer and he becomes reflective, in sharp contrast to the animated emotions displayed while recalling his experiences as a teenager.)

"I felt very isolated at Oliver High School. It wasn't like the white kids were racists. They weren't. But you have to understand the setting. The school didn't even have a black assistant principal. We were trying to relate our lives to what was going on in the world of civil rights marches, sit-ins at lunch counters, black power symbols, and we were regarded as troublemakers. We, in turn, didn't see ourselves as troublemakers. So they, the white kids, reacted to our behavior as did the school administration. They didn't view us as being oppressed at all.

"We were told to take the SAT tests, to score higher, to do this and that. And we were rebelling. We were not told of alternatives like the black colleges which would take us in and *prepare* us for the SAT tests. These colleges knew we would have to take these tests, but they would get us ready for them. You might be there for five or six years because they knew some problems had to be corrected.

"I'm talking about places like Shaw, Hampton, Morgan, and St. Augustine and other black colleges. They took you in, sat you down, and told us the reality that we, right now, were not where our white counterparts were. And this was not a put-down! They told us that we shared the same objective of getting a college degree, but it may take a little longer. This is quite different from being told you rank 212 in your class and will never catch up, as we were told at Oliver High School. There has been quite a change. Now Helen Faison (the Pittsburgh School Superintendent) is being rewarded by the same system that rejected her candidacy several years ago.

"We were in the business of trying to save this city. So while Oliver High School has changed, so has public housing. When I was in high school, public housing was integrated. Despite some definite changes, the society and the system have not changed. When I came to Oliver in the sixties, Franklin Park was all woods, and Cranberry Township didn't exist. Now, while Oliver has become a predominantly black school, Franklin Park and Cranberry Township are all white. So while in some ways some things have changed, in other ways it hasn't changed at all.

"It is a question of economics. It's a question of controlling the quality of life so that people will spend money, regardless. It is only when you allow quality to diminish that you find yourself in difficult situations. Pittsburgh once had a population of 600,000 and 10,000 public housing units. We now have 360,000 people, and we still have 10,000 public housing units. We also have a lot of other housing units that are out there for poor and moderate income people to choose from. Our products are becoming obsolete. Unless we shift to developing products that are not public housing, but are affordable housing that fixes up neighborhoods and are products that people want, we will become obsolete.

"Schools are no different. Unless schools understand and involve themselves with universities, businesses, and communities, and become more creative, they will also become obsolete. Because people will walk with their pocketbook, I think it is more a problem of economics than race.

"Here in Pittsburgh we are at the edge. We are in a race for survival. Six years ago we were on the verge of financial ruin. This was when Tom Murphy became mayor in 1994. But it's not about the city anymore. It's about the region. Given the population base we have, and given the opportunities that are out there, it has to become a shared experience in terms of resources and talent. Unless Allegheny County and the City of Pittsburgh share much more than they have in the past, we are not going to make it. It's not just a question of affordable housing, it's about rebuilding neighborhoods. When we ask about education, it's about integrating educational systems with universities, with library systems and with other school systems. It's not so much a matter of being integrated as it is a matter of providing the best education possible, and to make it available to all the residents and to *all* the students.

"We may have to do something like they did in Chicago and in Boston and say everything be damned! The old system must go, and turn the school system over to the mayor. Quality is all important, and ultimately it's a leadership issue."

Helen Faison

The Pittsburgh school administration building is a classic four-story granite structure reminiscent of the Gilded Age. It has withstood decades of use and retains its dignified appearance. Located in the Oakland section of the city, it is surrounded by the University of Pittsburgh, the Carnegie Library, Carnegie-Mellon University, museums, and concert halls. On the second floor is the superintendent's office, carefully maintained and efficiently furnished.

Dr. Helen Faison has just concluded a meeting with two of her staff in preparation for tonight's meeting of the school board. She is a tall, distinguished woman with a commanding presence accompanied by a naturally warm personality. Dr. Faison was asked to come back to serve as acting superintendent when the former superintendent left earlier in the summer of 1999 to return to his native city of Mesa, Arizona, as the school superintendent. Accepting this request to assume the role of acting superintendent after her retirement as deputy superintendent clearly indicates her love for the city where she was born and served as a teacher, high school principal, and central office staff administrator for many years. She certainly did not need the job, yet it was a sacrifice made willingly.

"I was born in Pittsburgh, started as an elementary school child, and then my mother became ill with tuberculosis. She knew she wasn't going to live, so she took us to Virginia to help us get to know her mother well, knowing she would be raising her children. My mother lived less than a year, and I went to a school for black children. All Virginia schools were segregated, and I finished the seventh grade.

"This was as far as I could go, since there was no schooling for black children beyond seventh grade in most towns. My father was very unhappy to have me out of school and he arranged for me to attend a high school for black children in another town in the county held in the county courthouse. Because there was no way for me to travel back and forth from my grandmother's house to this school, my father made arrangements for me to live with a family in that town.

"I went to this school for two years, and then my father remarried and brought me back to Pittsburgh. I graduated from a Pittsburgh high school, and two days before commencement my father died. I was the oldest of three children and there was no money for me to go to college. Fortunately, my high school French teacher took a liking to me and was able to get a senatorial scholarship that enabled me to go to Pitt (University of Pittsburgh). This scholarship, believe it or not, was one thousand dollars for four years. But I was able to get jobs after school and managed to graduate in four years with certification to teach history and geography. There was no job for me in Pittsburgh, since black teachers were not hired except in elementary schools and in special subjects. And those blacks with teaching jobs were nearly all in the Hill district.

"I finally got a job with the Allegheny County Board of Assistance and worked there until 1950. I had applied for a job in the city school system, and for whatever reason I got a job teaching at Fifth Avenue High School. In the 1950s, certain judges and prominent people in the city were pushing for the employment of black teachers, and I finally got a call. I taught English and social studies. Harry Singer became principal at Fifth Avenue High School and was like a mentor for me. I completed course requirements for school counseling and became the first black guidance counselor in the city. When Mr. Singer became principal of Westinghouse High School, I became vice-principal there.

"During Dr. Marland's tenure as superintendent in the 1960s, he selected me to be the principal of Fifth Avenue High School. This was in 1968, the year when Martin Luther King was assassinated. Oh my! What awful times. It was also the time of the Great High Schools plan, which was being discussed all around the city. Board meetings were news events and emotions were expressed openly. It was an incredible experience to be a principal in those years.

"At a staff luncheon in 1967, Mr. McCormick (deputy superintendent) urged me to get a doctorate. He said his one regret was that he hadn't. Well, I thought about this and decided to complete the requirements, including the dissertation. I took a year's leave of absence to work on the degree.

"When a new superintendent was hired, he reorganized the system and established three area superintendents. He asked me to be one of them. In 1980, Dick Wallace became superintendent and he contributed a great deal to the school district and to the city. I became a deputy superintendent in his administration.

"Going back to the Great High Schools, I must say it sounded like a great idea initially. But over time it became nearly a joke. At that time, agencies like the NAACP and the Urban League were pushing hard for desegregation. And the state's Human Relations Commission had indicated we had to desegregate our schools. The commission had a lot of muscle in those days.

"As the city school population became more and more black, the idea of a metropolitan plan, like what happened in Louisville, Kentucky, began to stir discussion. In Pittsburgh we always had a very strong parochial school system, and this made a difference. But a regional plan including suburban and city schools has never attracted any significant support.

"In 1980, the state approved a plan that desegregated all of the middle schools. This plan was already in place when Dick

Wallace became superintendent. He implemented the plan but did much more to improve desegregation efforts. All of the high schools were approaching desegregation except for Westinghouse, Schenley, and Carrick. Carrick was predominantly white, while Schenley and Westinghouse were totally black.

"The state allowed us to continue with the enrollment at Carrick because of the distance required to reach it, and Westinghouse was left as it was because there wasn't a pocket of white population near the school. As for Schenley, they allowed us to create a magnet school that has become extremely popular. We established the High Technology and the International Studies Magnets at Schenley, which worked. And the numbers held, keeping that school essentially 50 percent white and 50 percent black. We have an excellent principal there, and the district poured lots of resources into the school, making it very high profile in the city. We installed the acclaimed International Baccalaureate program, which added another attractive option for students all over the city.

"As to school boards, I prefer an appointed board to an elected board. The elected board, which is what we now have, tends to have members who see themselves as representing a slice of the city. It's human nature for them to do this, and they need to represent their constituents. Of course this leads to trading and deal-making.

"One of the most serious threats to our public schools is the voucher plan, strongly advocated by our governor. Fortunately, he was unsuccessful in getting this plan through the legislature. It would have been devastating to us, and I don't believe people understood it. It's almost always associated with right-wing politicians. If vouchers are eventually approved, it simply means the public schools will be left with greater percentages of the most difficult children to teach. Concerned parents know where the good schools and teachers are. These are the parents who enroll their children in the best magnet schools, and they will flock to where they believe the best schools are."

August 26, 1999

Al Fondy

At the end of 10th Street, hard by the Monongahela River on Pittsburgh's south side, sits a brand new building housing the Pittsburgh Federation of Teachers. It is testimony to the leadership of Al Fondy, the Harry Truman-style president of the union. Fondy became its president during an eleven-day strike over union recognition back in 1968. Indeed, the then superintendent's refusal to recognize the union made possible Fondy's election.

For more than three decades, the PFT has grown from a minor player in the city to one of significance and respect. Previous superintendents and the current acting superintendent all praise Fondy's cooperation and vision.

In his impressive corner office overlooking the river and the city, Fondy offers brusque, straight talk, free of educational jargon. He reminds one of Jimmy Hoffa because of his short, husky body, but even more of his former colleague, Al Shanker, because of his ability to go beyond his own constituency and embrace the needs of the entire city. His strategy is pragmatic, his tactics effective.

"When I became president of the union in 1968, the 'Great High School' advanced by Dr. Marland was in full swing. We finally came down against it. It wasn't so much the steep cost that defeated the plan. It was a bad idea. Can you imagine bringing five to six thousand high school kids together at one school? It certainly would have integrated the schools, but it would have been a colossal error. Fortunately, it never happened. Now there's no doubt that smaller schools are better.

Kids feel more secure and can achieve an identity easier in small schools.

"Prior to the 1960s, Pittsburgh had segregated schools, largely because of its three rivers and ethnic neighborhoods. There was a certain amount of integration based upon where people lived. They were three black communities—the Hill district, Homewood, and the Northside. Few blacks lived in the South Hills. So we were essentially a segregated city with some schools being 100 percent white and others 100 percent black.

"The State Human Relations Commission in the late 1960s made certain demands on the district to desegregate, and this led to different plans. We (the union) supported integration because we believed it was obviously a good thing. But whatever led to people moving away or sending their kids to private or parochial schools, that's not the way to go. We argued that ideally, kids should get together in kindergarten, first, second, and third grade, but that will require the maximum amount of movement of very young kids. This will produce the most resistance, and people will move away or take their kids out of public schools.

"The smart thing to do was to start the movement at the middle schools and leave the elementary kids in their neighborhood schools so they're near home. Focus on the middle schools for integration, and there will be less resistance. Of course, there was resistance anyway. When it was possible to change elementary feeder patterns to accommodate desegregation, we supported it.

"This middle school plan came after the Great High School idea, and the middle school, grades six through eight, was replacing the old junior high school. The middle school concept was sweeping the country and any resistance to it in Pittsburgh was strictly related to racial concerns.

"The magnet schools have helped to integrate the schools, and they seem to be working well. Of course, no one *has* to go to them, so they are not controversial. With all this stuff designed to integrate the schools, the reality is that the parochial schools, more than the private schools, severely hamper efforts to have an integrated system. There's no doubt about it. Too bad to say this, but it's true, and I'm Catholic. And there's no question that vouchers seriously threaten public schools. They simply divide people. The *last* thing you would do if you wanted to keep people together and less divided religiously, economically, and racially is to have vouchers. It is bad public policy.

"Overall, there's no question our schools are more integrated now than they were before we started all these efforts to desegregate. On the other hand, we have a lot fewer kids. Before all this started, we had close to 80,000 enrollment. Now it's around 40,000. Most of this happened in the 1970s. When Wallace (Richard Wallace) was superintendent, our numbers didn't change much—enrollment and racial.

"If the voucher movement fails, it's going to force some parochial schools to close or merge, and that would bring more kids into the public schools. And this is a good school system. There's no reason for people not to come to our schools.

"The school board is now elected by districts, so they are divided and very political. Bringing back Helen Faison as the acting superintendent was a good thing. She's terrific and commands respect throughout the city. (Helen Faison is a native of Pittsburgh, a former teacher, high school principal, and deputy superintendent. She retired six years ago.) Selecting the next superintendent will be extremely important.

"In thinking back on integration efforts, I remember the sensitivity training. It was garbage and insulting. They brought in some shock crap. It's B.S.! You don't convert people by insult. You work with them. You don't need that shock crap, it's unproductive. But I think that stuff has run its course.

"We have a stake in the schools. The better they are, the more job security we have. The union works differently now.

Oh sure, we must have decent salaries and be competitive. But we work cooperatively with the administration to maintain standards and have a good school system. It's a partnership.

"As to integration, everyone plays to his own constituency. We all do it, whether it's a union leader, an African-American leader, or an integrationist. But unless you move on and work toward agreements, you'll never accomplish anything. You have to balance your relationship to your constituency and try to move forward. It can be a tough balancing act.

"During these years of desegregation efforts, there were no mayors, no city council people who provided great leadership. They played to their own constituents. It was very hard to accomplish desegregation in Pittsburgh. If it were possible to go across the county line, it would have been easier, because you had something to work with—better racial numbers. Now you have African-American leaders calling for separate schools—separate but equal. What goes around comes around! It was never equal, and it isn't going to be. Some people would rather be a big fish in a small pond than be a small fish in a big pond.

"Look, I tend to be optimistic. I think this thing is winnable. Pittsburgh is making a comeback, a turn. What hurts us is the line between city and county. It makes us separate and enemies. A lot depends on whether people decide to move back into the city. There is new housing being built. Pittsburgh is not going to be like Newark (New Jersey). It's different, and it's vibrant. The new mayor (Murphy) is energetic and trying to move the city forward.

"The school system is a big asset. Look, do we have problems in our school system? Sure we do, but if you came in to analyze the city and took a look at what needs to be fixed, you wouldn't say the school system. Our school buildings are in good shape and always maintained. And there are good programs. The fact that the school system has its own taxing authority with the school board making its own decisions is terribly important. To make the school system part of the overall city budget would be a mistake. There is growing cooperation between the city and the school board as more and more recognition is given to the importance of its public schools."

August 26, 1999

Part II
Boston

Unlike the image of Boston during the busing crisis years, the picture in 2004 is remarkably different. Unsolicited positive comments came from city residents and from delegates to the Democratic National Convention.

Thirty years ago Boston, like other northeastern cities, had staunchly solid ethnic neighborhoods. Jews had left neighborhoods such as Mattapan and Roxbury. The Irish, now second- and third-generation, moved from the north end to South Boston, Dorchester, and Jamaica Plain. Blacks now occupied Roxbury, Mattapan, and the south end. Italians dominated the north end and East Boston. Chinese immigrants lived in a small area called Chinatown, which is now a major Asian area.

Years of fierce rivalries had developed between these ethnic enclaves. The annual Thanksgiving Day football games often ended up with fights and near riots, typified by the East Boston vs. South Boston games where Italian and Irish flags were waved.

Now, in 2004, there is significant mix. On Carson Beach in South Boston, blacks and whites stroll along comfortably. Even the L Street bathhouses off Day Avenue, named for Louise Day Hicks's father and the home of the traditional "Polar

Bears," are now used by all. Activist antibusing advocate Hicks would never believe the changes.

The 2000 census shows that Boston is a majority minority city with blacks, Hispanics, and Asians making up more than 50 percent of the city's population of 600,000. Immigrants from all over the world, including Russians, Middle Easterners, Asians, and many from African countries. Just look around such venues as the Charles River Esplanade, where the Boston Pops Orchestra gives free evening concerts, or the Faneuil Hall market area, and people of varying shades of skin color belie the opinion, still lasting, that Boston is a racist city.

Perhaps the best example is Bill Russell, the former Hall of Fame professional basketball player. He once characterized Boston as racist. He now says, "I think there are a lot of things that are happening to make it an open city where everybody is included, and there's nobody that's deemed unworthy." Russell helped promote the city during the Democratic National Convention.

The multi-billion dollar "Big Dig" has opened up the city, providing better access to the neighborhoods that earlier were difficult to reach.

All of the above descriptions help us understand why such violence and resistance to citywide busing became national headlines.

The Boston interviews with key participants during the 1960s and 1970s shed a sharper light on what was going on in Boston during those years.

Tracy Amalfitano

Tracy Amalfitano still reacts emotionally when recalling her experiences in Boston during the 1970s. Little wonder! Living in South Boston, believing in desegregation, accompanying her young son to the bus stop in "Southie" where he boarded a bus to the black neighborhood of Columbia Point, she paid a heavy price for her beliefs and courage. At certain points in her interview, tears welled up and recovery moments were necessary before she continued her story.

Tracy grew up in Maine and moved to Boston in 1949. She went to Boston University, met a man who became her husband, and moved to South Boston in the 1960s. She lived for thirty years in a typical "three-decker" house so familiar to Boston neighborhoods. Now working with the Boston Police Department as the assistant director of the Neighborhood Crime Watch Unit, she is continuing in her efforts to bring people together. A modest woman, she reflects the emotion of personally experiencing painful times.

"I remember vividly an incident that occurred one or two months before the judge issued his court order, the spring of 1973. My husband was with a client from the drug rehabilitation program and the three of us went to pick up my son at his school on the corner of Fourth and L Streets in Southie. I got out of the car and noticed a group of women selling buttons inscribed with the words 'No, No, We Won't go!' One of them came over to me and pushed me, saying, 'How come you won't buy a button?' I replied that I wasn't interested.

"I was always considered an outsider in South Boston. You know, I wasn't born there, didn't grow up there, and I married into an Italian family.

"When the plan came out with the judge's order, I found out that my son was going to be bused over to Columbia Point and the McCormick School. So I decided to go to the open house and look around, see what it's like. And I met the principal, who was terrific. I think he's one of the finest principals in the city, Mr. Bergen. From day one he was a big supporter of the parents. It wasn't threatening to him to have a mixture of parents from Southie and black women from Savin Hill, Dorchester, and Columbia Point. A group of us decided to meet during the summer, and along with Mr. Bergen, vowed that there wasn't going to be any violence when school opened in the fall. None of us realized how crazy it was going to get later. We were very proactive.

"I lived on East Seventh Street in Southie, and I knew I was going to take my kid to K and Marine Road. A lot of stuff was going on, and I began to get angry. 'What do you mean, everyone is going to boycott?' I said. 'I'm not going to boycott.'

"Well, the first day of school just me and my Michael walked down to the bus stop. And my son was the *only* one on the bus! Oh, I got jeered every day. There were motorcades, placards, and everything else going on to protest. Everything changed in my life. I was the only white from South Boston who was a member of the Parent Advisory Group. It affected my family—my husband's family disagreed with me.

"A lot of people were watching me, following me, and threatening me. Parents were afraid to send their children, but I felt very strongly about integration, and so did my husband. I supported the judge. I got a call from Lurine Morris, a black woman who was part of the Roxbury Cadre, an advocacy group of strong women from Roxbury that included Ellen Jackson, Ruth Batson, the Snowdens. This led to my being on the Social Advocacy Committee of Family Service for Greater Boston. So I went to meetings at Freedom House in Roxbury, and these black women were so valuable and supportive of me. (She now breaks down and cries. After twenty years, the memories are still so vivid that she is overwhelmed.)

"Later on, I became a target and began to receive threatening phone calls. My car was smashed! There was so much going on at South Boston High School. You had the T.P.F. (Tactical Police Force), police on horseback, motorcades protesting, boycotts going on, and I'm down at the bottom of the hill with my kid! The real story has never been written. As good a writer as Lucas (J. Anthony Lucas) is, he never got it right.

"In December of 1974, I got this telegram from the U.S. Commission on Civil Rights. It scared the hell out of me. It said 'You will report to Julius Bernstein's office on 27 School Street.' What is this! At this time, Bernstein was the Director of the Jewish Labor Committee and chairman of the State Advisory Committee for the U.S. Commission on Civil Rights. He was an absolutely marvelous person, and I guess I was asked to come to his office because I was sending my kid to school and they had heard about me.

"Some of Boston's most noted civil rights leaders were at this meeting, and I was extremely honored to be there with people like Ellen Jackson, Ruth Batson, Paul Parks, Dorothy Jones, and Evelyn Morash. This was a big deal for me.

"In the second year of the plan, we were all at home, and I was babysitting my nephew on the living room couch. It was a warm fall evening, and the second floor windows were open. Suddenly there was this commotion and noise. I looked outside and saw a bunch of young men with rocks and bottles. At that moment a rock came through the window and missed my nephew by about an inch. This was accompanied by a lot of obscenities, and it was over—quickly. The FBI came to my house, and I then began to feel that I was the perpetrator of something terrible. I asked myself, 'Why am I sending this kid to school?' And then I'd say, 'Why shouldn't I send my son to this school?' Those were hairy times."

August 21, 1997

Ruth Batson

Talking with Ruth Batson in her apartment on Cambridge Street in Boston, across the street from Massachusetts General Hospital, was a powerful experience. Her place is comfortable, "lived in," and her warm personality envelops the room. Few have had more consistent and active involvement with urban public schools spanning several decades. Now in her 70s, she retains her enthusiasm fueled by a deep sense of inequity.

"All my life I have been aware of the importance of education. As a little girl, my mother would point to her head and say to me, 'You've got to get an education.' While still pointing to her head and said, 'What you have in here, no one can take away from you.' She raised me and my brother and made clear to us that schooling was essential.

"Probably my earliest awareness of being segregated was in the 1930s when we moved to a public housing project (Orchard Park). It was completely segregated and later gained notoriety as Boston's worst housing project. But it was still better housing, and we frankly didn't care if it was segregated.

"It was while living in this project that I began to discover the terrible conditions of the Roxbury schools. I was invited to a meeting by an 'Avon lady' who belonged to a group called Parent Federation. The group was all white, so I was the only black present. The focus of the meeting was the deplorable situation of the Roxbury schools. Well, I became a regular attendee and my concerns grew. After all, I had three kids in those schools.

"Around that time I heard about an organization that was opening an office on the corner of Mass. Avenue and Tremont

Street. It was the NAACP. So I got myself together one day and rode the trolley to take a look. After voicing my concerns, I was told that there was an education committee, but it dealt only with scholarships and helped kids to plan and apply—stuff like that. I said, 'How are they going to get to college if they go to lousy, run-down schools and don't know this, that, and the other?' The response was that they didn't have any other approach, but would keep in mind what I told them. Well I came out of that place so mad! Here is the organization that calls itself NAACP, for the advancement of colored people, and they can't come up with anything better than that! Shortly after I got back home, I received a phone call from the man I spoke to at the NAACP telling me that someone had overheard our discussion and suggested that I form a sub-committee that would deal directly with Boston public schools. My answer was yes, and this took over my whole life. I often tell people that I went to the university of NAACP. This is where I learned everything. I hadn't been to college, and I learned how to write reports, give presentations, testify at the statehouse, and teach. All of this happened in the 1950s and explains how I got started.

"Boston's schools were segregated and certainly not equal. Our reports pointed out how unfair the schools were to our kids. One thing led to another until finally we reached our limit of frustration. At a meeting of the Boston School Committee (board of education) in 1963, our committee and supporters refused to leave the committee room and just sat in our seats. I remember Louise Day Hicks shouting, 'Don't point your finger at me!' She and her four cohorts on the committee were vehemently opposed to desegregation and had done nothing to comply with the law resulting from the Brown decision.

"Shortly after this experience, a committee was formed that included Leon Trilling from MIT, Bob Sperber (superintendent of schools in Brookline), and others. This led to the formation and start of METCO. (METCO is a program that buses inner-city African-American students to neighboring suburban school districts. It has been very successful in gaining state support and now has a waiting list of more than 1,000.)

"The years have flown by but I am discouraged. Racism still thrives. After all these years of struggle, we still have some of our schools threatened to be not accredited, inequality, and neglect. At least there seems to be an awareness that racism is alive and well.

"There used to be an old lady who lived on our street, and she would walk by our house. My mother would always greet her with a cheery greeting—'Good morning, how are you today?' She always responded, 'I feel defeated!' And I'm sorry, but that's exactly how I feel today. The key is power and who has it, where it is. If you have individuals like we do in Boston, with Jim Kelly as president of the City Council who says things like, 'Let's off Tom Atkins' (a former African-American member of the City Council and a mayoral candidate) during desegregation discussions, how can we be optimistic? Later on, in a newspaper interview, in an aside to a black reporter, Kelly asked, 'Would you want your daughter to marry a white?' Or take Peggy Davis Mullen, another member of City Council who is much younger. She is pushing hard for neighborhood schools, which would destroy whatever remains as desegregated schools.

"Now I am sure there are many people who I admire that do not reflect racism, but it all depends on who has the power. I truly felt we were going to succeed, but I underestimated the hate of the white people. How do you get past that? People just don't know enough of the facts. That's why education is so important. At least METCO is strong. But it hard to be optimistic, and the future discourages me. Everything seems worse. Poverty is deeper than ever. It's not just education that needs attention—it's the whole society and the growing divide between classes."

November 1, 1996

Carolyn Chang

The U.S. Office for Civil Rights in Boston is located on the 18th floor of the John F. Kennedy building in the government center section (formerly Scolly Square). Its atmosphere is relaxed as regional manager Carolyn Chang tells how she became involved with civil rights issues and school desegregation.

Government bureaucrats are viewed, often inaccurately, as mindless automatons who carry out regulatory tasks unimaginatively and prepare boring reports. Ms. Chang does not fit this stereotype. She is thoughtful and flexible in her assignments. She believes firmly that government must serve people.

"My parents are first-generation immigrants coming from China in the early years of this century. My father was about twelve years old, so he actually went through the public schools in Boston and became very fluent in English. But my mother never really learned English, nor did my relatives and their contemporaries, unless they were born in this country.

"I was the first one in my family to be born in the United States, so I'm second generation. As a teenager—maybe even younger than that but as the oldest daughter who could speak English—I was drafted to go along with aunts and cousins to interpret when they went to see a doctor or needed to go shopping or buy a major appliance.

"Because my father was one of the few English-speaking adults in the neighborhood, he was often called upon to be a spokesperson for a family association or a local Chinese organization.

"So I think it sort of was natural that I joined other people who were in my situation—second-generation Chinese-Americans who could speak English—in helping to become a bridge between the Chinese community and people in the wider community. Over the years the community grew, and people became U.S. citizens and began to register to vote. This attracted political candidates to our neighborhood who began to pay more attention to our community. We started to get involved with campaigns, and if the public health department needed to come down and do TB screening, they would call on people like me to help.

"As the community continued to grow, especially due to the change in immigration laws in 1965, the social needs outgrew the community's capacity to take care of them, and I think this corresponds closely with the civil rights movement in the late 60s and 70s.

"The Chinese community in Boston decided that it could identify needs and advocate for services as other ethnic neighborhoods were doing to help their members. So several of us started meeting and we formed the Chinese-American Civic Association. This became an umbrella group for other Chinese organizations, like the Chinese-American Health Association, the Chinese-American Education Committee, and so on.

"It was around 1968 when I applied for the position of manager of the Chinatown City Hall, one of the little city halls established by Kevin White when he was mayor of Boston. It was a very exciting time for me because we didn't have a lot of social service organizations prior to that in Chinatown. And we became actively involved, forming committees and dealing with issues. For example, we started the Chinese Education Committee, and I was active in the campaign to get the Massachusetts Transitional Bilingual Education Program enacted. That was back in 1970, so I guess that's sort of how I evolved into civil rights and eventually desegregation.

"I then went to work for the civil rights office in Boston. The office had already finished its work on Boston and the case was in the courts. It was during this period that the office started looking at other school districts in New England, so I actually did a lot of traveling then—places like Stamford, Waterbury, and Bridgeport.

"I remember the feeling we would get as we moved into school districts that had been cited for non-compliance or had received federal funds for particular programs. The Emergency School Aid Act was an example. It was one of those interesting ironies, since some of the school districts that applied for funding were not in compliance with the law.

"We were usually viewed as the enemy—as invaders. In order to receive money, you have to meet certain criteria: Was there a desegregation plan? Were parents involved? I mean there were specific stipulations. I really liked that legislation. It was well thought out. It set clear criteria for school districts, and it helped us know what to look for as enforcers. If you weren't doing the right things, you were not rewarded. I wish we had more legislation like that, speaking as a federal regulator as well as someone who wants to see some good changes.

"Waterbury was a tough little city. In fact, when our office first went there to do a review, they would not let us into the student records. Instead, they would have someone read the records to us. Can you imagine? We discovered that our notes didn't match with records. They were lying to us. We held up their money for a long time. It was an interesting kind of experience, because you would meet teachers, guidance counselors, directors of programs who on the one hand were glad that we were there but on the other hand couldn't be public about it—yeah, they were frightened.

"Connecticut has some very poor districts. It's sad. How can a state that has some of the richest areas in the country, if not the world, also have the poorest school districts?

"Hopefully, we are changing. I'm not sure we are there on attitudes, but certainly we are changing behaviors, and the way people in power carry out programs. This can lessen the adverse and unequal racial inequities. I think people are more conscious or cautious, and if they want to discriminate, they have to be more creative.

"Yet I think we've taken a step back (since the days of the civil rights movement), because I think, unfortunately, we've had leadership nationally and locally that have allowed or created an atmosphere where people thought it was OK to go back. What we need is more leadership that says *no*, that is *not* acceptable. That's *not* the American way.

"Where did we make mistakes? I don't think we focused enough on the quality of education. I think we focused more on putting people in the right boxes, and I have always felt very uncomfortable about that because it's not where you put the boxes, it's what do the boxes look like, what is in them. You have to look at the facility. You have to look at the teaching staff. Then you can work on things like attitudes or whatever, and then you have to be tough enough to take the right sanctions, too!

"I think you have to get the whole community involved. Education is something that needs involvement of a whole community. Now there appears to be good involvement with business and schools, and we could have done more of that in the beginning. The quality of the schools is going to reflect on the quality of the community.

"What would have happened if it had not been Brown v. the Board of Education, but say Brown v. City Housing Authority? Would schools have remained so segregated? If housing had been available, there would not have been so much of a struggle. We would have had no need to move back to neighborhood schools. It's understandable why parents want to be nearer to their children, and we have to have housing that accommodates this. Middle class parents will not move back to the city unless schools are much improved. The problem perpetuates itself."

July 18, 1997

Muriel Cohen

Muriel Cohen is a journalist, now officially retired. She continues to write occasional columns for the *Boston Globe*. She covered the Boston schools and their struggle with desegregation for many years, writing in both the *Boston Herald* and the *Boston Globe*. Ms. Cohen grew up in Boston and attended its public schools before her college experience at Simmons and the Columbia University School of Journalism. She obviously knows well the city, its people, politics, and institutions.

Cohen recalls vividly the incidents and personalities that made headlines in Boston during the years when the dramatic stories about desegregation of Boston schools shocked the nation. A sense of sadness, even tragedy, is revealed in her comments.

"I remember doing freelance work at the *Boston Herald* in 1969 while attending the Radcliffe Bunting Institute on a scholarship, which also allowed me to attend classes at the Harvard Graduate School of Education. It was a very exciting time, and desegregation was on everyone's mind. When I finished the institute, I went to work as an education reporter for the old *Boston Herald* before it was taken over by Rupert Murdoch.

"At this time, Paul Houston (currently the executive director of the American Association of School Administrators) and Richard Green (now deceased and formerly chancellor of the New York City school system) were young interns at the Massachusetts State Department of Education. They were working with a young man named Charlie Glenn who had the primary responsibility for drafting a desegregation plan for the Boston schools. The hearings held by the state board were wild! Everyone came out of the woodwork. One Boston School Committee member called me into his office one time when the court was threatening to sue the Boston School Committee and said, 'What are we going to do? People of your race (Jewish) are supposed to be smart. Tell me what we can do!' Meanwhile, Kevin White (the mayor) was flailing around and pandering to the public.

"Desegregation tore the city apart in many ways. But fortunately, there were some noble and strong people like Tracy Amalfitano (now with the police department) and Nick Flannery (now a judge) along with others who did what they could to make it work. Tracy, for example, lived in South Boston and willingly sent her children on the bus to the black neighborhood of Roxbury. Flannery wanted to establish a metropolitan plan that would have involved 65 suburban communities. The judge ruled it out immediately, pointing out that he would have to deal with each one and that's impossible!

"A colleague of mine at the *Herald*, Ian Foreman, and I wrote a series of articles on 'metropolitanizing' the Boston schools. EDCO (Education Collaborative for Greater Boston) was an early example of a metropolitan approach consisting of seven school districts, including Boston and some of its suburbs, but there was strong political opposition to such ideas. For a short period the 'feds' provided money to support a metropolitan plan that included those communities in the Standard Statistical Metropolitan area of Boston, but this was short-lived. All this was happening in the early and middle 1970s.

"There was severe pressure on Judge Garrity, constant and from all directions. No doubt he had a liberal bent, and he was closely tied to the Kennedys. Around this time (middle 1970s), I got a call from the managing editor of the *Boston Globe* that led to a meeting with Tom Winship (*Globe* editor) and a job. Two of my new colleagues, Derrick Jackson, a black columnist, and Bob Healey, who was the *Globe's* guy in Washington, were especially insistent. Healy was also a personal friend of Garrity and how much influence he had on Garrity is only conjecture. In any case, I believe such influences pushed Garrity into premature decisions and led to the court order in June 1974. Even the schools didn't know what the plan was, and they were scheduled to start in September.

"The whole city was on edge, and Phase One of the desegregation plan was the main story hitting the front pages on Boston's papers nearly every day. Maybe, if Garrity had given them more time, the worst parts of the plan, especially the neighborhoods chosen to mix, might have changed, and more success achieved. But the clock was moving and the ill-considered plan was launched.

"It was awful! We were prepared to go, and had thirty to forty reporters on Day One stationed where we thought there would be flash points. Actually, on Day One there was no violence. And that's the way the *Globe* ran the story. No one believed us, and from around the country came charges questioning our reports. 'What do you mean, no violence? Come on!'

"People just expected Boston to explode on the opening day of school, and reporters from other cities were all set to report action. We were expecting it ourselves. Oh, there were a few incidents, but nothing like we thought. Overall, it was a quiet opening. On a scale from one to ten, it was about a two, and we were vilified by those who didn't believe us. I stick by my story. Of course there were those who didn't want things to go smoothly—politicians and others who opposed desegregation and saw their careers benefiting from negative results and racial incidents.

"There was a Haitian laundryman who got beaten up, and there were minor incidents in Charlestown, Hyde Park, and elsewhere, but given the landscape and the potential for serious violence, these were minor incidents.

"I think the black community behaved far more maturely than whites. If I were a black kid, I don't think I would have boarded a bus and gone to a school in a hostile neighborhood. Blacks could have gone on a rampage, and I would not have blamed them.

"We really could have had a race riot, and those of us on the scene expected much more to happen. Oh sure, kids were assured protection, and they were. But nonetheless, some students had to sneak or escape through a back door. It was hairy!

"At South Boston High School, where emotions were at a peak, there were incidents occurring inside and outside the building. But the trophy case wasn't touched. It was located on the second floor with all the awards and trophies displayed prominently and encased in glass. It was so vulnerable, but there was so much respect for 'Southie's' sports teams, it wasn't touched! Unbelievable!

"There must have been ten superintendents coming and going during those years. Take Bill Leary, for example. He meant well, but was caught between a scoundrel like John Kerrigan (school committee chairman) and an incompetent school administration, a bureaucracy that had built up over the years.

"Mistakes? Clearly, the first mistake was relying on that state plan, and pairing South Boston with Roxbury. They might have started just with the lower grades. The plan was faulty, the execution even worse. There was a lack of technical expertise in devising bus routes, and they were sabotaged by those who didn't want it to work. There was no strong leadership that made it unmistakably clear that they wanted the plan to succeed and were determined to make it work.

"Political leaders, the school committee and activists, thought they were going to stop the plan. The active sabotaging, the undermining that went on in and outside the schools, was constant. It has been a terrible, terrible learning experience for the school system, and I don't think it has recovered yet. It may never recover.

"There's an up side and a down side. Schools in Boston and other cities are suffering from poorly trained teachers and administrators.

"We have teachers who can't spell, can't speak grammatically. The bottom line is we are not getting good people, regardless of color. It is a most frightening reality. With Mayor Mennino, the political situation appears to be better. Certainly he is much better than Jim Kelly (currently president of the City Council). Tom Payzant (superintendent) is certainly smart, but I would prefer a stronger leader, someone like Bud Spillane, who was a natural here. You would go up to the Parker House and there he would be, wheeling and dealing.

"On the bright side, you have this new constituency coming into the schools and making itself felt. I see the Southeast Asians as the future hope of the Boston schools. I really do. These are people who are committed, hardworking, and who value education. If you pick up the paper in June, they are the valedictorians and salutatorians. And they do not care about racial differences, like black and white. It's not part of their culture. They envision the American dream."

Judge W. Arthur Garrity, Jr.

As he nears his eightieth birthday, Judge W. Arthur Garrity remains actively involved as one of the judges serving on the U.S. District Court for the District of Massachusetts. Recalling his experiences with Boston school desegregation was not difficult. His agile mind vividly remembers those days and the emotional events associated with them.

Once I gained access to his office in the John W. McCormick Federal Court House in downtown Boston, I found him alone, nattily dressed and warmly receptive to my questions. His informal but quite proper Bostonian responses were open and candid. We began the interview discussing the chapter on him in Anthony Lucas's book, *Common Ground*.

"Don't get me started on Lucas! Not that I didn't like him. He is a talented writer, and I was saddened by his tragic death. But he wasn't accurate, and I believe he had his story already written in his head before he started to write. It's like a novel with deliberately drawn characters playing roles he designed for them. For example, he claims I was named after Wendell Phillips, the famous New England abolitionist. Not true! According to my mother, my father's first name was Wendell due to my grandmother's fondness for a boy who used to deliver papers in the neighborhood. She probably never heard of *the* Wendell Phillips.

"But apparently, Lucas wanted to paint me as a "lace curtain" Irishman with 'Yankee Brahmin' pretensions. In any case, his account of me is filled with inaccuracies.

"At the time I was assigned to the school desegregation case in 1972, I had five or six hundred civil cases in my docket, plus a full load of criminal cases—maybe thirty or forty. In those days there were just six of us in the court, and we had no magistrate. I had but one secretary, and one law clerk. I say this because there was a certain amount of serendipity involved in the whole story. For example, I got this desegregation case through a lottery system this court uses to determine how judges get a case. They had separate drawings of slips with the names in random order, and my slip with my initials came out of the drawing. That's how it was done back in '72.

"We began with the so-called 'Masters Plan.' I talked with many possible masters—at least a dozen, starting with Thomas Pettigrew, a Harvard sociologist, and Paul Ylvisaker, who was then dean of the Harvard Graduate School of Education. They chose not to serve as masters, and I went for the team of Dentler and Scott, who were the dean and assistant dean of the School of Education at Boston University. Dentler was white and Scott was black. They presented a rather elaborate scheme involving a team of experts. The ideas were fine, but Marty Walsh (regional director of the Justice Department's Community Relations Service) knew the territory and helped me select four additional masters: Eddie McCormack, former Massachusetts Attorney General; Charles Willie, professor of education at Harvard; Jacob Spiegel, retired judge; and Francis Keppel, who had been a U.S. Commissioner of Education. They joined Dentler and Scott to form the masters team. We had several hearings and received hundreds of letters, most of them negative and many downright nasty.

"Now mind you, the State Department of Education had drawn up its own plan following the passage of the state's Racial Imbalance Act. Hearings on this plan were held in 1973, and I gave the School Committee an opportunity to present their own plan. The Supreme Court was no longer saying to desegregate with all deliberate speed, but to do it *now*. Here we were in June 1974, and schools were to be opened in September. Well, frankly, the state plan was all we had, at least in the first stage. And the Boston School Committee was not agreeable to any plan requiring busing. They were not only uncooperative, but actively stirring up opposition.

"When schools opened and crosstown busing went into effect there was some violence, a lot of disruptions, villains, and heroes. Neighborhoods like South Boston, Charlestown, and Roxbury, where Irish and blacks lived in solid ethnic zones, were especially affected. And I was the target for critics and much verbal and written abuse. It didn't bother me particularly, but it was a strain on my wife. We had twenty-four hour security for three and a half years. There were pickets coming out to our home in Wellesley, but there was only one serious threat when a guy came up to the house with an automatic rifle. He was crazy, a nut.

"Everyone wants to know if I have any regrets, made mistakes, or perhaps might have done it differently. It depends on how you view it. If you view it as the way it existed at that time, and the Supreme Court said that it wasn't a question of desegregating with deliberate speed, but doing it now, there wasn't much leeway. Under the law as it existed, I think what I did was consistent with and really required by the law. The case was appealed seventeen times and each time I was upheld.

"We might have done some things differently. Eddie McCormack, the former state attorney general and one of the masters appointed by Judge Garrity, thought that certain sections of the city with predominantly black residents, like Dorchester, would mix better with South Boston than kids from Roxbury, which was about 100 percent black. Dorchester, which once was largely Irish, still has a small Irish population and there would be less hostility.

"McCormack never conveyed that to me, frankly, until much later when the *Boston Globe* was doing an article on the desegregation plan. I said to him then, and would say it again, that if I heard that proposal and understood it, maybe I would think it a better arrangement. Certainly that's possible.

"There are other things that could have happened. We could have gotten greater support from political leaders. Ray Flynn (former mayor of Boston), who succeeded Kevin White, was a real asset; people don't know that. He was doing his best to eliminate the turmoil in South Boston High School. He'd be right out there on the sidewalk telling the kids 'Get in the school! Get your ass in there!'

"In reflecting on what happened in Boston twenty-five years ago, roughly, I recognize that I was of the old school as to how judges function. We never talked to anyone outside the court who might try to influence my decisions on a case. That was my obsession—a firm, firm rule—and I never depart from it. So when people would try to make submissions, I would say, 'Wait a minute. You can't do that! Kevin White tried to reach me in an effort to sort of broker the thing.' But coming from the background I had, I was so indoctrinated and committed to not having any ex parte communications with anyone. It's been sort of a religion with me, and I think maybe I was a little unnecessarily cautious or strict. Because I know of other cases where judges have talked their way through some of these desegregation cases and other cases by having one side in and then the other side. Perhaps I made a mistake by not being more of a mediator.

"What city has done the best job on this issue? It's probably the first case—Charlotte-Mecklenburg. Of course Jim (the judge) had a nice geographic advantage—there's a railroad track that pretty much runs through the center. And all the blacks are on one side and all the whites are on the other. So it was not so complicated and more logical than our situation in Boston.

"Another interesting aspect of the Boston case was how I lost my first black plaintiff lawyer. It's an indication of how views were changing, even back then in the black community.

"Larry Johnson was representing the blacks in the early stages of this case, and probably because of the obstacles and obstructionist tactics of the School Committee, he moved to a different position that was similar to the Atlanta approach, which stressed improving the resources and facilities serving predominantly black schools—more like separate but equal.

"When you ask me my opinion regarding the future of city school systems, there's only one answer. It's always: It depends. Of course, it depends on so many things. I would think principally on money, and whether the money is going to be devoted to schools is impossible to forecast. Schools are competing with other governmental needs. But perhaps if there is peace, and there isn't so much of our national resources devoted to the military? But, because schools have taken the place of other institutions in our cities and play such a key role in families and their needs, it is possible that school funding will become a national priority. Just to rehabilitate school buildings will require enormous sums of money. And now the costs of providing for the handicapped (special needs) is far beyond what the average person recognizes and those figures increase the average per-pupil costs. There are now so many different categories that qualify for support. Maybe there's an answer in technology and providing a computer for every kid. I guess I am pessimistic, really, about the future of city schools.

"I do believe that desegregation has done a lot to change behaviors and to improve the curriculum. But I want to emphasize I didn't do the politicking, the mediating work, that was required, because I truly had five or six hundred other cases. I just truly didn't have the time."

October 21, 1998

Charles Glenn

Perhaps the one person most familiar with the inside story of Boston's struggle with school desegregation is Charles Glenn, now a professor of education at Boston University's School of Education. He has a broad background of involvement with civil rights. He was jailed in North Carolina and marched in Selma, Alabama, during the 1960s. He was also active in the Massachusetts Freedom Movement during these years, thus he experienced a version of civilian basic training before his service with the Massachusetts State Board of Education.

In 1971, Glenn was hired by the then Commissioner of Education Neil Sullivan, well known for his leadership in desegregating schools in Berkeley, California, and in Prince Edward County, Virginia. His responsibility under Sullivan and Sullivan's successor, Greg Anrig, was to develop a desegregation plan for Boston and to ensure compliance by Massachusetts cities with the state's 1965 Racial Imbalance Law.

"Most people don't realize that considerable pressure was building against the inept Boston School Committee prior to the 1965 Racial Imbalance Act. The Boston chapter of the NAACP along with the Massachusetts Freedom Movement were demanding a wide range of improvements, including action to attack the racial isolation of African-American students. The School Committee strongly resisted any serious desegregation actions, insisting that there was no discrimination. One member remarked that 'We don't have inferior schools in Roxbury, we just have inferior students.'

"To be fair, Superintendent Ohrenberger did make some attempts to lessen the racial isolation through voluntary transfers by minority students and by building new schools in racial fringe areas where both white and African-American students could walk to school. But such efforts were mostly token and monitored closely by the School Committee. Call it stalling or whatever, but this was a deliberate tactic to avoid any serious desegregation plan.

"When the federal court found in June 1974 that Boston was operating a segregated school system, Judge Garrity ordered the state plan to be implemented in September. He had little choice! The Boston School Committee was now facing the reality of a desegregation plan they thought was avoidable. Indeed, rather than participate in the planning, they had spent the previous eighteen months preparing legal appeals, believing the plan was unworkable. So instead of working on modifications that would have corrected some of the defects of the plan, the school system had only a few weeks of the summer to prepare for major changes in school assignments when schools opened in September of 1974.

"Because the School Committee refused to cooperate and thwarted the administration, Judge Garrity found himself making more and more administrative decisions. It was a wild time that led to a succession of school superintendents. But one thing was a success. The school system was formally desegregated by law.

"Oh yes, the population change in the schools was dramatic. Before desegregation, white enrollment was about 70 percent and is now under 20 percent. To blame this all on desegregation is unfair. Undeniable population changes were occurring before 1970. The non-white student population doubled between 1960 and 1970—from 16 to 32 percent. Even in the close-in suburbs, the white student population was decreasing as the aging white population no longer had school-age children.

"What would I do differently if I think back about it? Well, for one thing, I would try much harder to work closely with local officials, especially during the early stages of the process. Although our positions were upheld by the courts, being 'always right' and they being 'always wrong' created a destructive atmosphere, when collaborative problem solving might have led to some solutions. We simply, because of past experience, distrusted the Boston School Committee.

"Thinking back, I admit that we were very concerned about how our actions (State Department of Education) would be judged by the country much more than how our recommendations would be received by the school system. On the other hand, I recall that under the leadership of School Committee Chairs Louise Day Hicks and later John Kerrigan, the school department officials were forbidden to meet with me. So maybe we would not have been able to work out solutions together.

"Another mistake we made was not to work more closely with parents. We just assumed that they would eventually overcome their prejudices and send their kids to the schools we selected to serve the common good. How arrogant! Allowing parents to have some choice, some say in where to send their children, could have reduced some of the tension and emotion. An example of this approach is when Judge Garrity permitted the school system to adopt a plan called 'controlled choice.' Professor Charles Willie of Harvard helped develop this plan, which was implemented in 1989, and it is now still in effect. It abolishes the former school attendance districts and requires parents to indicate their preferences of schools. Depending on school capacities and racial guidelines, parents receive their first, second, or third choice of school for their children.

"We established four information centers for parents and the staff of each school were helped to develop materials that explained their schools and programs to prospective parents. This new approach has worked quite well, and only roughly five percent of children each year are in schools not acceptable to parents. It is 'messier' than the former arbitrary and authoritarian system of assigning children, but the new approach has helped considerably.

"What we have learned through bitter experience is that rigidity is counterproductive. Being more patient, seeking solutions through a variety of channels, involving parents and teachers in making choices, and using the pressure of desegregation to press for educational reforms leads to more positive results."

August 15, 1997

Frank Jones

Growing up in a poverty-stricken small town in rural Mississippi during the Great Depression and moving to the big city of Chicago at age fifteen in 1948 provided a major culture shock for Frank Jones. The following interview was held in a townhouse in Boston's South End while Jones was running for a seat on Boston's City Council.

"I experienced absolute segregation and degradation as a child in Mississippi. Back then in the 1930s, integration was inconceivable—why, we had a great fear to even step on the campus of a white school! My father went blind when I was seven years old. He had been a porter on a train, and it was my job to take care of him while living with my grandparents in Mississippi. So I was absent from school a lot, but my grandmother taught me at home, probably better than the teachers in the segregated black school. It was an early example of home schooling.

"When I was fifteen, they sent me to relatives in Chicago, and this was the first time I ever interacted with white people. I went to high school on the west side of Chicago, and it was a racially mixed school—Jewish, Italian, and black kids. The faculty was all white, mostly Jewish, and McKinley High School was just beginning to change. Most of my friends were white kids, and it was generally a positive experience.

"In those years, there were three jobs that black kids could get that were considered to be good jobs—Pullman porter, post office positions, and the third was teaching in a segregated school. Following high school I went into the army and this was another segregation experience, even though the armed forces were desegregated by President Truman in 1948. It took several years before the order was implemented.

"You know you spend your whole life fighting the idea that you are inferior. In Mississippi, we got our books from a depository that distributed books white kids had already used. I remember distinctly three things I learned in Mississippi. They taught us that studies of blacks in World War I showed a higher rate of incidence of black veterans with venereal disease so we were considered morally inferior. Then studies of IQ tests concluded that blacks were intellectually inferior, not taking into account that only recently had they been off the plantations. And study of medical records revealed that blacks had this strong tendency to have sickle cell anemia, so they were considered physically inferior. Morally, intellectually, and physically inferior! That's what we were taught, and it was devastating. It gets embedded in your mind.

"I went into the army when I was seventeen years old and served in the 101st Airborne Division. We were getting ready to go to Korea, but I had this bad eye, which I eventually lost, and was honorably discharged in 1950.

"After attending junior college, I transferred to Chicago Teachers College, which was integrated with Chinese and black kids from the projects. I became a teacher at the Williams School in Chicago, and at that time race was not an issue. For six years I taught and went to school at night, gaining my law degree in four years.

"With my law degree, I became a lawyer for the NAACP in 1963–64 and went back to Mississippi. I found little change there with one significant exception. People were now challenging the system. To have indigenous people who had been subjected to segregation and inferior positions willing to challenge Jim Crow laws was truly meaningful.

"This was when many whites came down to Mississippi to work with blacks on voter registration and other civil rights activities. I remember working with Marian Wright Edelman at that time. She had just graduated from Yale and not yet gotten her law degree. I was in Philadelphia when Sheriff Rainey was in office, and when Goodman, Schwerner, and Chaney were murdered. It was an exciting time, but I was really frightened in those days.

"I came back to Chicago and worked with legal services. Then I went to Washington, D.C., to work with the Department of Health, Education, and Welfare when David Tatel (now a federal judge) was heading the Civil Rights Division.

"In 1980, I served as counsel for Community Services Administration while Carter was president and was involved with investigating the riots in Miami in 1980. We all thought Carter would be reelected and I saw opportunities in Boston. There had recently been a shooting of a Charlestown High School football player, busing was still stirring resentment, and racial tension was high. Kevin White, then mayor of Boston, had called for a committee representing the major institutions of the city to address racial tensions.

"*The Boston Globe* was represented, the president of the first National Bank, Cardinal Medeiros, and others. I felt if we could demonstrate that a city, on its own, could be successful in dealing with these racial issues, it would benefit the whole country generally and specifically other cities. For six years I worked on this project, and we made some progress.

"Certainly racial tension still exists, but not with the same intensity. The demographics of Boston are changing with a growing black middle class and significant increase of Asian and Latin American people. Economically the city is experiencing a major comeback. Just what will happen with the schools remains to be seen. Now the mayor appoints the superintendent, and the current superintendent, Tom Payzant, is making some changes. We'll see what happens."

October 19, 1997

(Frank Jones has retired and does community service work.)

Jean McGuire

In sharp contrast to a typical corporate office, Jean McGuire's is cluttered, filled with files of newspaper clippings, magazines, bookshelves jammed with books related to race matters and history, plus file cabinets stuffed with records of students and school systems that have worked with METCO, the Metropolitan Council for Educational Opportunity. METCO, which is funded by local and state monies, has bused African-American students from Boston to surrounding suburban school districts for more than thirty years.

Ms. McGuire was born in Boston in 1931, the daughter of a man whose father was a former slave. This grandfather arrived in Victorian Boston in the late 19th century. He married an Irish maid and this marriage produced eight children.

"My dad was born on Beacon Hill, my grandpa in Virginia on General Robert E. Lee's plantation. Daddy still lives, despite all kinds of ailments. He has survived tuberculosis, cancer, arthritis, eye and ear problems, and much more. I am going to see him this afternoon, and he is truly remarkable at ninety-nine years of age. He went to Prince School on Exeter Street, dropped out of high school and joined the Navy in World War I. He came back, graduated from high school, and went to Bates College.

"So you can see why education has played such an important role in my life. And I went to all-black schools in Boston and Washington, D.C., where I lived with my grandmother in Georgetown. She lived in a row house with no running water or electricity. But she recognized the value of education, and after graduating from Dunbar High School, I went to Howard

University. Before going to Washington, I went to the Dearborn School in Boston and to Girls' Latin School. I took the classical course, hated Latin, but benefitted from it. Following my graduation from Howard I went north again and received my master's degree from Tufts University.

"All this schooling led to teaching and counseling kids. So I was well prepared to take over METCO and the controversies surrounding it. Actually, it would cost the participating school districts significant money if they dropped the program because of the state reimbursements they receive through their participation. The kids and the adults all benefit from the program. Oh sure, we have our share of problems, but overall there are positive educational results that go far beyond standardized test scores.

"I do get concerned about young people's lack of a sense of history. History is like a skeleton, but with muscles, blood, nerves, in addition to bones. If you don't know where your feet are and all the connections that eventually reach your head, you won't understand the relationships. But I'm not too worried about the young people; they'll be OK. My husband, when talking about our daughter and her white boyfriend, says, 'I don't care who she is sleeping with so long as he's going to pay Blue Cross and Blue Shield—and takes out the trash.'

"If you are a black American—or anyone who is a minority—in your life experiences you inevitably get involved with discrimination. One way or another, you encounter it. You don't have any choice. The system has ways to make you feel no good. We've been through slavery, lynchings, poll taxes, all kinds of stuff. There is always some kind of a struggle, even getting a job. But I always ask, 'Did you register to vote?' I want to make sure young people know they have a voice, and that you do not have a voice if you shut up! It reminds me of Barbara Jordan. What a president she would have been! If only Jimmy Carter had the courage to put her on the ticket. She had this profound respect for the Constitution and for democracy. I can still hear her now when she spoke at the Watergate hearings.

"No, you can't give up on one kid, even those who get into serious trouble, like this METCO girl (she points to a picture). Someday soon she is going to be a parent. Kids must develop a sense of values. Your charge as a public official is not to give up on a kid, to make sure kids have an opportunity. They are not formed yet, but what is cheaper—thirty-thousand dollars or a year in jail? (At this point in the interview, Leo, the custodian enters the room and she had him talk about his daughters. One is a physician, the other a school principal. When he left the office, he was beaming with pride.)

"There were several racial incidents involving our kids in suburban schools—yearbooks, for example. Under the METCO kids' pictures would be code letters like I.N., which stood for Ivy Niggers. And this was in liberal Concord in the early 1990s! In Braintree (a suburb south of Boston), they had a local chapter of Louise Day Hicks's old organization called ROAR—Restore our Alienated Rights—and they would terrorize our kids. METCO buses would be greeted with jeers like,'Hey, blackies!' But this has been true throughout our history with minority groups. Remember the World War II chant—'Chinkie Chinkie Chinamen eat dead rats.' When we lived in Canton, our electricity was pulled during Christmas time. They didn't want niggers living in Canton.

"All this kind of stuff was always an onslaught on your psyche. I can see why people have high blood pressure. People take things for granted. You know you are an American when you go abroad and visit countries that don't have storm drains, sidewalks, bridges, telephones, radios, TV, on and on. And you realize how lucky you are. We have so much—50,000 choices in our stores! This is true, but if there is shoplifting going on, who is first suspected?

"Oh yes, there have been major accomplishments resulting from desegregation. All that Jim Crow stuff is gone legally. The tenor of our times is very different from the days of the Brown decision. What was said openly then may be thought, not spoken. What is slower to change are the assumptions that lie behind segregation. Behaviors have changed because laws have changed, although earlier assumptions are still there. This is true also of women—like the idea of a woman president. There is still the feeling that blacks can only dance, sing, and play ball well. There are assumptions about 'those' people. Any people can have this assumption. Actually, everybody was involved in the slave trade. There's a little black in everyone. You find these things in all cultures.

"It is all about power and who has it. And it is a question of how power is used. Take teaching, for example. A good teacher knows how to use power. Like the saying goes, 'Children don't care how much you know until they know how much you care.'

"As long as you take the public's money, you have to give everyone their 14th amendment guarantees, their rights, their equal opportunity and guarantee to equal access.

"Right now there is no way avoiding what the METCO kids have to do. After all, people drive a long way to get to their jobs! One of the white boys in Lincoln (a western suburb of Boston) said, 'You find out through METCO that all black kids don't dance, or sing, or play basketball well.' And one of the black kids said, 'You find out that all white kids aren't smart and can't all spell.' You learn to judge people first as individuals, not by stereotypes.

"School desegregation leads to better understanding. Whites find it difficult to be a 'nigger lover,' but friendships are formed, and they last.

"People live in two worlds. There's probably not one black family in America that goes through a day when there isn't something to do with race that comes up. Race is the biggest fiction in the world. It makes me so angry and it is a tragedy. The world has so many problems and to have decisions made based upon race is a great tragedy. Gwendolyn Brooks talks about 'one mighty drop.' Thank you, Mr. White Man, for making so many of us.'

"But really, why shouldn't the white kid, the black kid, the Spanish kid, the Asian kid, all learn together? It's realistic!"

July 17, 1997

Bill Ohrenberger

Interviewing Bill Ohrenberger was a sad but engaging experience. Here is a man who is in the Boston College Football Hall of Fame; he was also a track star in his youth during the 1920s. Now he has great difficulty moving his still large frame, having had hip replacements and other operations. Well into his eighties, he retains an alert mind full of memories. He lives with his daughter in Situate, Massachusetts, often referred to as the Irish Riviera.

"I loved every minute of it! Being superintendent of schools in Boston during the early years of the desegregation movement wasn't easy, and much of the criticism was undeserved. The alleged segregation of the Boston schools was never deliberate.

"Kids went to the high school in their district, and they probably went to the junior high school in the same district. Children went to the school nearest their homes, and if the housing was segregated, so were the schools. Unlike the South, schools were not intentionally segregated.

"Boston was probably the only city that had kindergarten classes *and* pre-kindergarten programs. This is common now, but not when I was the superintendent.

"Oh yes, there were heated protests. I remember hundreds of people waiting outside my office building on 15 Beacon Street waiting for me, and the police led me out the back way, through the library, to get out. Some mornings it was necessary to have the police escort me out of the building just to get through the crowd. One lady was screaming and kicking and she thought she had kicked the officer, but she actually kicked me. But I made no indication of her mistake. I told the officer 'you just got a theoretical kick, but I took it!' It was an awful time, and we were doing everything we could to remedy the intense feelings.

"I remember when a national committee (National Advisory Committee on Civil Rights) came to Boston, and it was headed by Father Hesburgh of Notre Dame. I overheard him say to Arthur Gartland, a member of the school committee, 'I can't wait to get Ohrenberger on the stand.' That I didn't appreciate—he was prejudging me.

"Boston was not as bad as some cities where major rioting took place. Judge Garrity's plan came after I retired in 1972. But the state was pushing for desegregation and passed the Massachusetts Racial Imbalance Law in 1965. (This was the first state law against *de facto* segregation.) Owen Kiernan, the State Commissioner of Education, was a real leader, and it was the Kiernan Report in 1965 that led to the Imbalance Law. He, unlike many others, understood the big cities. There was a lot of naïveté. Judge Garrity tried to run the schools, but you can't do it part-time.

"We began busing to relieve overcrowding, not to desegregate. When I was superintendent, if I could have had the money spent on transportation to support the busing plan, I could have spent it on improving schools throughout the city. The mistake made was in the assumption that if you just mixed people arbitrarily, you would help everybody. In my opinion, if they had to rewrite the law, it would not be as drastic. The plan caused havoc within families, because where before the oldest in the family, like the big brother, would walk his sisters and younger brothers to school since they were all in the same district. Under the Garrity Plan, you could have four children from the same family going to schools in four different districts. This led many families to private and parochial schools. And I think it also led to increasing delinquency.

"One thing that happened as a result of desegregation was that people began to realize the problems big cities had. We began to understand better the problems of others.

"Schools were asked to solve all the problems. It's impossible! I'm afraid it is going to be impossible to support city schools, because it will be too costly. Nobody wants to go to a run-down, decrepit school."

Gary Orfield

If one were to name a writer/scholar most connected with school desegregation, it could be easily be Gary Orfield. Now teaching at Harvard and formerly at the University of Chicago, Orfield has done an enormous amount of research on school desegregation and continues to participate actively in the debates and struggles over the issue.

His office at Harvard's Graduate School of Education is a beehive of activity with a constant flow of students and phone calls creating an atmosphere of excitement and serious engagement with topics relating to politics and education. Orfield is comfortable and well seasoned in his role as an academic activist.

"While growing up in Minneapolis in the 1950s, I became extremely interested in what was going on in Little Rock and in what was happening in the South. I was about ten or eleven, and I used to pick up all the newspaper coverage. Carl Rowan was then a reporter in a Minneapolis newspaper and did several series about what was happening, and had a substantial impact on me. This was Hubert Humphrey country, a good place to grow up. When I went to college at the University of Minnesota, I was still a Republican moderate because of my family's background.

"I got involved in politics very early when Richard Nixon was nominated. That moved me to the Democratic Party, which I joined when I was a freshman in college in 1960. It was an amazing time, and during my college years the civil rights movement was at its peak. Many of my friends went down to demonstrations in the South; some of them ended up in jail. Our

Congressman had to go out and get one of my friends out of jail in Georgia where he had been arrested for criminal anarchy.

"My own activism at the time was directed at problems in Minnesota. I was running the student government and became very interested in racial issues in general. That whole experience was a powerful influence on me in the sense that it made me realize what poor people are really up against, especially poor minority people who were facing economic devastation and very intense prejudice. And in Minnesota it was especially directed at Indians, even more than African-Americans.

"I wrote my senior paper at the University on Little Rock and Oxford, Mississippi, and how the administrations had handled it. So nearly all my education is in political science.

"Benjamin Willis was the Chicago Superintendent of Schools while I was at the University of Chicago, and there was a tremendous battle going on in the 1960s. I used to go to the school board meetings, which were frequently fascinating, and they became increasingly contentious. Willis was a real segregationist, and would run down the back stairs of the school to avoid being confronted by protest groups. And when I was in graduate school, the government cut off federal funds for Chicago over the issue of segregation. It was the first time this had ever been done, and five days later they were forced to give them back because of all the political pressure. Anyway, the whole process got me interested in thinking about federal civil rights enforcement, which turned out to be my dissertation and my first book. All of this led me to the segregation issue and to a powerful, divergent kind of career.

"By 1972, my wife and I had moved to Washington, D.C., and we sent our first child to the local public school. We were living on Capitol Hill in a mixed neighborhood where there were a lot of young white families who would either move out of the city when their children reached school age or send them to a private school. Our daughter had a wonderful kindergarten teacher and she had a fabulous time in school. So we organized the neighborhood, formed a large co-op babysitting arrangement, and recruited a lot of families into the school. And it became an integrated school after it had been virtually all black.

"Well, the whole dynamic of the neighborhood changed. We had an active parent association, and it was a wonderful experience. The school became 30 percent white and multi-class. The hardest people to get involved were middle-class blacks who were overly pessimistic about the D.C. school system. But this became a great school and really brought the neighborhood together in lots of ways.

"One of the things I discovered from this experience was the powerful effect it had on the teachers. It had appeared to be a completely awful school, but it had some wonderful teachers who had become discouraged. Once they knew they had strong parental support, they came back to life. It was fascinating to see the enthusiasm grow. I remember a second-grade teacher who I thought was not very good when I first met her. She turned out to be wonderful, and one time she came over to our house and said, 'You know, Mr. Orfield, I haven't had a parent come in to say anything positive to me for fifteen years!"

"It has become much harder for cities to attract bright kids to teach. In earlier times the only place for young black professionals to get a job was in the cities. This is no longer true as interracial suburbs are recruiting them for their schools. Our family had a lot of good experiences with integration. Our kids went to excellent public schools, both in Washington, D.C., and in Chicago.

"I've learned a lot about the structure of our society, about the various institutions, and how to change them. The basic issues are not that complicated. We've known for at least a couple of decades how to make schools work and how to help integrate schools. The problem is the lack of any long-term political support for doing anything seriously about racial problems. And the intellectual community hasn't been very interested in bringing about serious change. The understanding that we had developed during the turmoil of the 1960s has not been sustained. So we should be pessimistic about the leadership we've created in this society in the last generation. But we shouldn't be cynical about our young people. They are much more optimistic, helpful, and want to work on projects. I have many gifted students who are excited about urban issues, and they are anxious to get involved.

"What do I think is the greatest accomplishment of the desegregation movement? Well, we got rid of the apartheid system in the South and we had a South Africa in our country. It was a comprehensive apartheid system and it's gone! Now that's an accomplishment! I felt that was the basic goal of the civil rights movement, and it was pretty much accomplished in about five years.

"After that was accomplished, it became apparent to almost everybody who was involved that the next issue was urban inequality, and the problems related to schools, housing, and employment. It turned out the country wasn't going to do a damn thing about these areas of discrimination. And there was a tremendous political reaction that brought Richard Nixon to power and the whole conservative movement. Racial fears were stirred up, and terms like 'forced busing,' 'governmental interference,' and 'loss of liberty' became popular and distorted the goals of desegregation.

"In the next decade so much is going to depend on the courts and where the balance lies. If the courts continue to move to the conservative right in its decisions, much will be lost. I think the initiative taken by President Clinton on race is a small but an important step. It's been a very long time since we've had a serious discussion about race.

"As the demographic changes in the country begin to take hold, different kinds of political coalitions will become possible.

And with these developments happening, there will be social ramifications leading, perhaps, to major changes. Younger people, especially young Latinos from California and Texas, are very conscious of the fact that they're going to inherit this society in a certain way. And we have to pray that the society will change in the way Nelson Mandela has changed things—with graciousness, compassion, and understanding, not with the revenge and counter-racism that is our greatest risk."

July 21, 1997

Paul Parks

One hundred Boylston Street in downtown Boston, where I interviewed Paul Parks, is on the edge of Boston Common and the Public Gardens. Curiously, it happens to be the location where I first met Paul Parks in 1968, when the Education Collaborative for Greater Boston was being formed. Back then, he was a key player in the struggle over school desegregation, and he remains actively involved to this day. His ethnic background, African-American and Seminole Indian, caused him to be a victim of racial discrimination, but initially in a different way.

"I lived in an all-black neighborhood in Indianapolis and was regularly teased by black kids because I looked different, coming from a Seminole father and a half-black, half-Seminole mother. There was one white family, and one of their kids became my friend. We needed each other for protection.

"One of the things I never forgave myself for was asking my father to change the way he dressed, because he used to wear moccasins and his hair was worn like an Indian. I remember how he looked sternly at me and said 'I will not change the way I am for anybody. I am proud of what I am. I am a member of the Seminole nation. Why would I ever change what I am? I am proud of my heritage.' He taught me a great deal, and told me to keep in mind who I am and to never criticize a person for something they can't do anything about. This training was extremely valuable, for it made me feel I never have to feel badly about my background.

"Race is a phony concept. We come from ethnic groups or nationalities really. And suddenly, when it becomes a matter of sons and daughters of former slaves, we talk about race. The very term African-American indicates that this person has black or brown skin. We need to eliminate the idea of race. The current NAACP convention should deal with this, but they won't, because it helps them to use it. Actually, they could overcome all the issues concerning race like Colin Powell, politics—all economic, housing, and educational issues. There is no logic to the concept of race, and to make a value system out of something that has no basis makes no sense. We can begin to readjust how we look at each other.

"So you can understand how I became involved with desegregation and education. My mother also had a great influence on me. She used to push us, all the time, to do well in school, to pay attention. She was very ambitious and valued education. It was a way of breaking through barriers. Well, I must have paid attention because I did well in high school and went to Purdue University where I got my engineering degree. My high school in the black neighborhood of Indianapolis was very interesting. It was named for Crispus Attucks, the Revolutionary War hero, and had an enrollment of 323 kids. All but twelve went to college. Can you believe that?

"As a young man I came to Boston to follow up on a job application to the well-known engineering firm of Stone and Webster. Young black engineers were a rare commodity in those days (the 50s), but to my surprise they hired me.

"Over time I became fairly well-known in Boston and had a variety of interesting assignments. Back in the late 50s, I was a member of a citizens group and we were trying to change the school system. Ruth Batson was running for the Boston School Committee, and she called me to ask if I would join her NAACP committee that was attacking *de facto* segregation in the schools.

"This led to a continuing involvement with Boston's schools and education generally. I was a part of the group that pushed hard to desegregate schools in Boston. No, I did not participate in the sit-in at the School Committee meeting in

1963. It reminded me of one of my father's sayings: 'Don't put your oars in the water unless you intend to row the boat.'

"I remember being investigated by the FBI at the time of the Model Cities Program when I was Secretary of Education for Massachusetts. We had been receiving millions of dollars for education and this agent said to me, 'We are going to get you!' and I replied, 'Take you best shot.' Nothing ever came of this.

"I never was intersested in making money—never dreamed of it. This took place during Reagan's administration when there was a backlash against desegregation efforts. Ed Meese was the U.S. Attorney General and I was supporting Jimmy Carter.

"But, to go back to METCO, I think that one of the most brilliant things we did was to get the State Department of Education to support the program. This has made it possible for every school district that participates in METCO to receive state funding. There is now a per capita head tax for each Boston student that goes to a suburban school. So, in addition to the state aid they already receive, these suburban systems get additional money from the state. And do you know why METCO stays alive? Because suburbs would lose money if they dropped out.

"At the time I was chairman of Suburban Fair Housing. And my Boston friends said to me, 'Why get involved with that? There are things here to do in Boston.' I replied, 'Look, we have here a constituency, and my mother used to tell me if you are going to have a constituency, you'd better include folk who have ability and who do not look like you.'

"Billy Bulger[1] used to get so angry with me. He would say, 'Look, I have a problem with school desegregation because it is changing my community. South Boston is not going to be what it used to be, and I dearly love South Boston. I hate to see it change—people are leaving.' I replied, 'I see what your problem is. You're like a fortress, and you live within that fortress. That's your turf. And if somebody else comes in, you run to the ramparts to repel the invaders. This was your land, your schools, your bars, your streets, and now you have to share.'

"You can't ask poor people to share. And when those buses came into South Boston, it was much more a matter of losing their community than anything else. Actually, they had very little to share. South Boston was even poorer than Roxbury, and poor people don't like to share because they have so little. I recommended that Roxbury be paired with West Roxbury, a predominantly white middle class neighborhood. But Judge Garrity said to me, 'Paul, back off. The state department has developed this plan and we are going ahead of it.'

"What they did was to take two poor, very poor, white communities—Charlestown and South Boston—and ask them to handle one of the most difficult, complex social problems in the country. I said to Judge Garrity, 'I think you will rue the day, because I think this thing could work, but not the way it's being planned now.'

"It reminds me of my association with Louise Day Hicks, who was chairman of the School Committee during this time. We actually developed a good relationship. I remember being asked by Roxbury citizens to have Louise Day Hicks come to Freedom House in Roxbury to meet with parents. I called her and convinced her to come to Freedom House and that I would pick her up. Sure enough, she came and listened to black parents complain about schools and the problems of their children. On the ride back to South Boston, she said to me, 'Paul, I've got to do something about these conditions, and I will!' Well, a short time later she called me back and said, 'Paul, I'm sorry. I just can't do it.' I asked, 'What do you mean, you can't do it?' She replied, 'Gillis (then the superintendent) called me in and said if I go ahead with my plans to help Roxbury, you will never win another election in Boston.' And it was Gillis, not Hicks, that caused the mess in Boston. He was retiring and on his way out, and he did not want to change the way things were. He was the villain of the story. Gillis was the enemy of school desegregation. Hicks's political career would have ended if she didn't capitulate."

(Paul Parks was formerly Massachusetts Commissioner of Education and is now serving on the State Board of Education.)

Note

1. For years, Bulger was the most powerful state legislator, representing South Boston. He is now president of the University of Massachusetts.

Tom Payzant

Tom Payzant was born in Boston and after experiences as a superintendent in various locations across the country, he is back in his native city as its superintendent, assuming the position in the summer of 1995.

His first involvement with a major city was in New Orleans in 1967 when he left the Harvard Graduate School of Education to be an assistant to the superintendent. Since that initial administrative assignment, he has served as a school superintendent in Montgomery County, Pennsylvania; Eugene, Oregon; Oklahoma City, Oklahoma; and San Diego, California. In San Diego he led the school district from 1982 to 1983. Before returning to Boston he served as Assistant Secretary for Elementary and Secondary Education in the U.S. Department of Education. His career covers more than thirty years. This experience gives him a broad perspective of desegregation and its impact on schools.

"Early on, I was motivated by inequity, and New Orleans was a vivid example of it. When I arrived in 1967, the city was in the initial stages of desegregation. They had what was called a 'Freedom of Choice' plan where students submitted their choice of school to the central administration. The superintendent took over this plan; I still remember stacks and stacks of white permit forms. The inequities existing in New Orleans were so obnoxious! Huge gaps existed between white and black schools on all levels. Black schools were in horrible condition, and most schools, including white ones, had no air conditioning. My time in New Orleans was short, but valuable in solidifying my awareness of inequality.

"My first superintendency was in suburban Philadelphia, where I caused quite a flap when I proposed an exchange program with Philadelphia schools. White resistance was immediate and strong. Moving from the east coast to Eugene, Oregon, was an interesting experience largely free from any racial issues. Eugene at that time was a university town and predominantly white.

"Oklahoma City was a classic case where one section of the city was black and the rest white. The lines were clearly drawn, although a small Asian population lived in the city along with a small American Indian community. White flight had already started, and the student enrollment had been reduced to 47,000. At its peak, Oklahoma City had about 75,000 kids in its public schools. One-way busing led to this white flight and efforts to retain a more racially balanced school system were failing.

"When I arrived in San Diego in 1982, there was already a court order for desegregation, but the city had its own voluntary plan. The court had identified a number of racially isolated schools. These were turned into magnet schools to achieve racial balance. But new ground was being broken in San Diego because the court also established achievement goals in the schools that had been identified as racially isolated.

"There was less white flight in San Diego due in part to the *voluntary* plan. Although there were expectations regarding racial balance; it was a gradual process. Not all schools were immediately desegregated. Really, it was a combination of factors that enabled San Diego to be more successful than some other cities. First of all, San Diego encompasses a large geographic area, and over time there were changing patterns of population. Establishing magnet schools, the voluntary desegregation plan, the size of the city geographically, and shifting neighborhood populations all worked to slow down white flight.

"Coming back to Boston reminds me of the difference between eastern cities and San Diego. For example, Boston's ethnic groups have a longer history of isolation. Neighborhood patterns have been more resistant to change; generations have grown up in essentially the same areas. And Boston is much smaller geographically. What are suburbs to Boston would be part of the city limits in San Diego. One of the wealthiest sections of San Diego is La Jolla, and La Jolla High School has (by choice) 30 to 35 percent of its students from the poor barrios of the city. It is considered as one of the best high schools in the country and the kids who are bused there matriculate through the school as successfully as those who come from more advantaged homes.

"So Boston is quite different, but it is undergoing some interesting changes. When I came back to Boston in 1995, I inherited Chuck Willie's controlled choice plan. As to whether it's working or not depends on one's point of view. About 10 percent of our students do not get their first or second choice—or really any choice—and they represent a highly vocal minority that is highly dissatisfied and angry. Yet about 80 percent do get their first choice. It is significant that the quality of the school as perceived by parents determines choice more than the school's location.

"Overall, middle school parents are generally satisfied in Boston. At the high school level, 72 percent choose a school's program and reputation over location or a neighborhood school.

"There has been a lot of white flight in Boston over the years, but now it is more a matter of economic class, and black middle class families are part of the 'flight' that used to be overwhelmingly white. Here's what happens in Boston: A high percentage of white parents will send their children to kindergarten and then take them out because the Catholic schools do not have kindergarten. Then when their children reach sixth-grade level, these parents will have their kids take the exams for the three secondary exam schools—Boston Latin, Boston Academy, and O'Brien School of Science and Technology. If they make it (pass the exams) they will send their kids to public schools. If not, they won't.

"There has been some movement back but not a significant number. Our current enrollment is now 63,000 and the increase is primarily due to in-migration and a small degree of families moving back to the city. Over the last few decades, there has been a swing from the high 80s in the 1960s to the low 50s in the 1980s, and now we raised our enrollment to 63,000.

"I don't think there was any way else to begin desegregation following the Brown decision but to physically move kids by busing. In hindsight, and I want to emphasize hindsight, we should have concentrated much earlier on the education quality of schools and achievement standards. We missed an opportunity, and this was a mistake. We needed to pay more attention on access to opportunity and looked closer at the results. It wasn't until the late 1980s that schools separated out test scores when the significant gap was revealed between ethnic groups. If we had done this early on, we might have been able to stem some of the flight. And we still are not sufficiently aware of how race and class intersect.

"It was never really the bus ride that was the issue, because parents who have been able to exercise choice for their children have been transporting them to where they believe quality programs existed. In my view, as people become more open-minded about race and are able to tolerate diversity, what will determine where parents send their children is the quality of the school's educational program.

"If we had known that mandatory busing was going to result in major white- and later middle class (both black and white) flight from major cities, would we have done it the same way? It's very hard to generalize, but of the experiences I have talked to you about, there was less white flight in San Diego and that was, in part, because of the voluntary plan and the judge-set achievement goals in minority isolated schools.

"When you have a number of ethnic groups it is less likely to tip. When there is more diversity—a variety of ethnic groups rather than just two—there is more chance of success. If you had roughly 25 percent white, 25 percent black, 25 percent Asian, and 25 percent Latino, you would see more stability and parents hanging in. This is borne out by my experience in Oklahoma City.

"In terms of accomplishment, I think the desegregation movement has been rather remarkable. When you stop and think about it, there have been only two institutions over the last fifty years in our society that have been asked to take on the tough job of moving from a segregated to at least a partially integrated institution—public schools and the military. And had the other institutions of society—the churches, synagogues, the private sector—take any institution you want—been part of the desegregation effort, we would probably be a lot further along than we now are. The widening of the economic gap between the haves and have-nots has made it more difficult, and this has been especially felt in the 80s and 90s. The impact of poverty is profound and a major factor.

"I think there has been a lot of progress in terms of students' attitudes. In our metropolitan area, there are now students from various ethnic backgrounds going to school together. Folks have made their way into the middle class, and the growth of the black middle class is significant. Here in Boston I think we will go ahead with choice. It does attract people and retains diversity."

November 1, 1996

Bob Peterkin

Bob Peterkin is now a professor of education at Harvard's Graduate School of Education and directs the Urban Superintendent Program. Before this, he served in various positions—teacher, high school principal, and superintendent of schools. All of this experience in cities like Albany, Boston, Cambridge, and Milwaukee gives him a perspective and insights that are valuable in assessing school desegregation.

Growing up in New York's boroughs of Queens, Manhattan, and Staten Island adds to his knowledge of urban areas and their schools.

"Queens was the first time I ever attended a segregated elementary school that was overwhelmingly black. Even though I grew up in three boroughs of New York City, only in Queens did I attend a segregated school. In Washington Heights in Manhattan, it was predominantly Dominican, but there were blacks, Jews, and Italians all mixed in. And that was in 1959.

"In high school I went to mostly white schools as my parents had moved to Staten Island. So the issue of race was felt more by neighborhood than by schools, and our friends at this time were across the spectrum. I went to college at the State University of New York at Albany. At that time I'll bet you there were 3,000 students and maybe twenty of us were black. This was the early 1960s, and it would not be an overstatement to say that I knew all the black people on campus.

"So I didn't really confront desegregation much until Boston. My first teaching experience was in a residential treatment center for severely mentally disturbed children. This was around the time of the civil rights and the black power movements, and I became involved with young people—black adolescents, mostly boys. We got involved in what we called the Black Heritage Program. Psychologists called it a counter-conditioning program to help kids feel less isolated on racial issues and with their emotional difficulties.

"The first sense of desegregation as a major component of the business of public schools didn't come on my screen until June 21, 1974. That was the day I was appointed Headmaster of Boston English High School and the day when Judge Garrity handed down his court order demanding desegregation of Boston's public schools. English High School was going to be a new school, and throughout the two-month process of interviews, no one mentioned the desegregation issue.

"I remember flying back to Albany (where he was serving as principal of an alternative school). I have the *Boston Globe* and the *New York Times*, and both papers have the picture of Judge Garrity handing down the orders that call for desegregating Boston schools by September of 1974. The news carried stories about possible violence and resistance. John Kerrigan (a very vocal foe of desegregation) was the School Committee chairman and he and Louise Day Hicks were pictured with Hicks shouting, "Never, never, never!"

"In Boston, they referred to that day as 'Black Friday,' and they appointed three black principals on the same day.

"Well, you may remember we opened schools on time and violence happened immediately at other places in the city. We dodged this pretty well until October 8, 1974. I remember all these days. It was a painful period of time—exciting, but still painful. This was the day after Ted Lansmark had been attacked on City Hall Plaza with that flag and had his nose broken. Black kids were angry, as were the white kids, and they went after each other. We're talking about a limited number of kids, and there were kids in the building who never knew we had a riot because English High School was a ten-story building and they were up at the top half of the building. They were returning from a fire drill and went upstairs. But outside a few words were passed and then it started.

"We had a plaza of about an acre right across from Boston English School and police were parked all around. We were trying to get the kids back inside after a fire drill—actually a false alarm. Oh yeah, kids used to pull false alarms all the time as a tactic to get out of school, start fights, and do whatever they were going to do. And we had a riot. It can't be described as anything else. A thousand kids were outside punching each other while we attempted to break it up. Now the cops joined the fray and I was knocked to the ground.

"Later on we figured why it had taken so long to come to a boil. Remember, this was a month after school had started, and we had lived through a reasonably quiet period of time. We didn't get our student assignments until just a week before school opened, so we had kids sitting in the auditorium while we scheduled them by hand for the first two weeks of school. It was a volatile situation that was heightened by the reassignments of many kids, blacks and whites, who didn't come to school until October. This led to territorial disputes and increased tension.

"I tried to do some bridge-building in West Roxbury (a white section of the city) before school opened. I was asked to speak to a small group of parents in West Roxbury who were concerned about their assignments and who didn't know anything about the new English High School. So I got together a slide show, brought along my two assistant headmasters, and headed out to West Roxbury.

"I proceeded to go through the whole thing of what the school could offer: a brand new twenty-five million dollar building, an Olympic-size pool, art studios, music practice rooms, and more. And probably 10 percent of the audience nodded their heads and thought this might work. There were lots of questions about safety and security as well as some ignorant comments. But I think they were impressed by the fact that I came with two assistants, stayed, wasn't afraid, and stuck around after the meeting to talk to people. If you stand up, you'll usually get a few advocates. So these folks sent their kids to our school and formed a nucleus of support.

"If you remember, ESAA (the federal Emergency School Aid Act) provided funding for urban schools dealing with desegregation and diversity. What a shame that Congress killed that legislation! Anyway, we used some of that money and got white and black parents to come together, meet, and talk about what we would be doing, visit the school, and meet in each other's homes. They formed our parents group and sent their kids. With the help of ESAA we had fifty aides inside our building and yet we still had a riot. But remember, South Boston High School had the National Guard, state troopers, and the local cops, and they were having fights every day.

"We *had* to figure out a way to get these kids interested in being in our school. So unlike other high schools in the city, we did not cancel fan participation at the basketball games. We were determined to have dances, and we did. We were determined to have clubs and student government. Instead of having elections, which would have been racially charged, we invited anybody who wanted to be in student government. We wound up with 200 kids, and it was largely accomplished by young black and white teachers working with students. Despite the riot and fights, we still had a nice prom and the white and black kids who were calling each other 'niggers' and 'honkies' were hugging each other and crying at graduation.

"We became a magnet school under phase two of the desegregation plan, and during our second and third year, people were flying into Boston from Milwaukee, New Orleans, and other cities to look at us. Boston was the first large city to really go through this.

"The magnet team enabled us to expand our partnerships and programs. For example, the vice president of John Hancock Insurance Company showed up one day and he turned out to the best buddy I've ever had. He hung in there with us, funded teachers, and just did yeoman service. And another partner was the University of Massachusetts of Amherst, where I got my doctorate. They worked with our faculty and helped us with the curriculum.

"So we became a magnet school focusing on the arts. That led to 'partnerships' with the Massachusetts College of Art and Brandeis University's Theater Arts Program. We actually had four or five options for kids to choose from. In addition to the fine arts and theater arts program, we also had medical careers and urban studies programs. So you can see a lot came from our connections and partnerships with business, universities, and the professions. All of this attracted a mass of students who really wanted to be there because of the program options and a lot of good teachers.

"English High School was a place kids wanted to be, and we were largely successful with a truly mixed student body. I think this says a lot for what can be done in bringing together kids from widely varying backgrounds and providing an education for them.

"Looking back, there were some humorous moments. In our first year, 1974–75, we had all those false fire alarms—about ten a day! Well, you know the elevators and escalators shut down when the fire alarms goes off, and you can imagine walking up and down ten flights of stairs. It only takes about two of these before people get angry. Add the bomb threats being called in and you reach a point where you either have chaos or you ignore the alarms and bomb threats.

"I finally turned off the fire alarms and stationed aides on each floor to report any possible fires. The Fire Department came over and said, 'You can't do that!' I said, 'More kids are getting hurt flying down the stairs than if they were fleeing a fire.' So after heated verbal exchanges, I was handcuffed, and the superintendent intervened to prevent them from taking me to jail. After explaining our temporary solution, the Fire Department signed off on the logistical plan and came to talk to our staff that would be in charge of the plan.

"They actually committed $250,000 to install a delayed system over the next summer. It may seem like a little thing, but unless this action was taken, our school would have lost hundreds of kids, since we would no longer have control of our building.

"Unfortunately, after the third year, things began to regress as the school system began to cut back in funding and we had to lose many teachers who had been hired specifically for our programs. As the riffing (reduction in force) process went on, more senior teachers—those with more years in the system—replaced the younger and less experienced teachers who were 'connecting' with the kids and who had a stake in the programs that had been developed. The senior teachers tended to be more militant and inflexible. What had been an encouraging start for a new school during an extremely difficult and emotional time in Boston was now being lost. A teacher strike at the time just intensified the problems.

"I was at English High School for three and a half years. We went through a period when several superintendents came and left—four from within. They all stood tall, in my opinion, but were working under a School Committee politically committed against busing and desegregation. They refused to cooperate with efforts to obey the court order, and only with a new School Committee and a superintendent hired from outside the system, Robert Wood of the University of Massachusetts, was some progress made.

"Coming in from the outside, Bob Wood did not feel swallowed up by the desegregation order. It was there, and it's 1978, and he had to deal with it. But he was the first one who started to think about extricating the system from the order. He wasn't consumed by the desegregation issue, and he didn't feel the pressure as his predecessors did.

"This school system (Boston) and this city are still consumed by desegregation. Cab drivers rant about it, and it's always right under the surface. Was desegregating the schools wrong? As a concept, certainly not. Clearly, mistakes were made, and when you're one of the first major cities out of the box, they were glaring.

"The Boston schools were allowed to deteriorate for decades, but the magnet school approach was a positive idea so long as the programs are strong, of high quality. Parents are not going to send their kids to school just to meet desegregation numbers. With the controlled choice plan that requires a certain percentage of racial balance, the schools with quality magnet programs are attractive to parents of high school kids.

"The 'exam' schools (where students take a test for admission), like Boston Latin, Boston Latin Academy, and the John O'Bryan School of Mathematics and Science, are popular—especially Boston Latin. If I'm not mistaken, more than 50 percent of the white children on the high school level are in those three schools, and 51 percent of the white children in the Latin schools come from parochial schools. The feeling is that if you don't get into the 'exam' schools, you're stuck with mediocre district high schools.

"We have to make these plans as voluntary as we possibly can, i.e., controlled choice. And the programs must be well developed and the schools have to be held accountable. This has not been done in the past. It's hard to say what will happen."

August 7, 1997

Bob Sperber

Bob Sperber is now professor of education at Boston University following a career in educational administration. For eighteen years he was superintendent of schools in Brookline, Massachusetts, an inner suburb surrounded by Boston and the city of Newton. Before this he served for three years in Pittsburgh, Pennsylvania, as the assistant superintendent for personnel.

Raised in the Bronx, New York, Sperber is thoroughly urban oriented and has dealt for many years with racial and urban issues. These matters still motivate him. Listening to this concerned educator relive his experiences reveals a caring and discouraged man. As he leans back in his chair, bald head glistening, a sense of calm determination is evident.

"My first involvement with school segregation goes back to Pittsburgh. When I arrived in this northern city in 1961, the faculty was segregated. Black teachers taught black kids and white teachers taught white kids. I felt that was wrong, and we went ahead and systematically convinced black teachers to accept assignments in white areas and began to desegregate the faculty. We also brought to downtown headquarters the first black administrator in central administration.

"During my early years as a teacher and administrator, I was generally aware of inequalities existing in northern public education, but not intensely so. But in Pittsburgh, where it was more blatant, my awareness was heightened.

"Then I came to Brookline and to a community that was actively engaged in civil rights matters. I remember one of my earliest school committee meetings (in Massachusetts, school boards are called school committees) when the Brookline Civil

Rights Committee came and expressed its strong belief that Brookline should do something to relieve the poor learning conditions for minority kids in the city of Boston. Viola Pananski, chairman of the school committee, appointed Leon Trilling, a professor at the Massachusetts Institute of Technology, the chairman of the Brookline Civil Rights Committee, me, a parent, and some kids to form a group to look into what we might possibly do. We made contact with Ruth Batson and Paul Parks, community activists in Boston leading the fight for better education for African-American kids. We had a meeting in Brookline and the conversation turned toward the possibility of Brookline and perhaps other suburbs opening up seats for Boston kids—African-American kids. Trilling began making contacts with leaders and school committee members in nearby suburbs and a working committee came together. Harvard's Graduate School of Education was also involved and working hard to get Boston to participate with its suburbs on educational projects.

"And so out of all this emerged what became METCO, the Metropolitan Council for Educational Opportunity. We got a grant for three years from the federal government to do some planning, and in 1965 we selected Joseph Killory as our first director of the program. He was succeeded by Ruth Batson, then by Bob Hayden, and ultimately by Jean McGuire, who still runs METCO.

"When we first started this program that buses Boston kids to suburban schools, our expectation was that the program would be temporary and provide some relief until such time as something more permanent in nature took place in Boston. And in fact, the suit to desegregate Boston public schools ultimately moved to Judge Garrity, who in 1974 ordered Boston to desegregate its schools. Interestingly, the METCO program is still going on today, thirty-two years later, and is still oversubscribed. These Boston families voluntarily subscribe to this program.

"Right after the school committee endorsed the idea of accepting Boston's students to Brookline's schools. I was summoned by the high school faculty during the 1964–65 school year. The faculty asked why I would even consider doing something like this because it would obviously lower the school's academic standards. They felt it would not work, that it was artificial—you know, all the typical arguments. And I listened and responded to their questions and then finally I said, 'Ladies and gentlemen, we have been together an hour or two, and I just simply want to let you know that this is something we're going to do, and if you're uncomfortable with this, then your recourse would be to leave this community and go to a community where they are not going to do this.' And there were no takers. They all stayed, and so we launched the program.

"I was also involved with another project designed to bring city and suburbs together through programs that would pair a suburban school with a Boston school, do joint science projects, exchange students and teachers. All of this represented a form of desegregation. We called it the Metropolitan Planning Project and received federal grants to support it for a few years until a Congressman from Grand Rapids, Michigan, who later went on to become the 38th President of the United States (Gerald Ford), succeeded in stopping the program. He felt it was a threat to the suburbs outside Detroit." (Author's note: Along with the cessation of funding of metropolitan planning by school districts came the 1974 Supreme Court decision in the Milligan v. Bradley case that severely limited lower courts' ability to order suburbs to join with cities in desegregation plans. This was the first defeat for civil rights in twenty years.)

Hand on his head and stretching, Sperber begins to reflect on school desegregation: "I think it's been a failure. Not because the white families left, but because the Boston schools never improved. And it's been a failure because they never did what they were supposed to do, which was to ultimately integrate.

The more important part is to actually bring people together, give them an opportunity to learn to know one another and respect one another for their abilities—and that never took place.

"Boston never tried seriously to integrate. The courts had to order them to desegregate. Louise Day Hicks and John Kerrigan (former chairs of the Boston School Committee) did all they could to prevent desegregation. They were essentially venal people. They blocked busing, and then when the court ordered it, they ran against it as an evil someone else caused.

"The system has really failed these kids, and they now probably spend thirty-five to forty million dollars a year busing kids from one end of the city to the other in a school system that now has fewer than 20 percent white kids. It really at this point makes no sense.

"Yet in spite of the sad Boston story, school desegregation makes clear that under the 14th Amendment, people have an equal opportunity to get educated wherever they want. That is a basic tenet in our Constitution, and it has to be applied equally to all races. So that's a major accomplishment. But I am not convinced that it ever did what it was supposed to do, and that was to ultimately end up integrating our society. I mean that was the original purpose of the public schools. That's what made America such a unique place—that here was an institution that was structured so that all of the people with different backgrounds and different religious and economic standing and racial differences could all come together, get to know each other, learn together, grow together, and as a result really produce a strong, vibrant country. And that's not happening. The racial divisions are, in my judgment, just as severe as they have ever been.

"Looking back, from hindsight, I guess I would have looked harder at solutions other than busing kids from one neighborhood to another. Parents just physically find it difficult to become associated with a school that's not close to their own neighborhood. Better magnet school programs would have been one way to desegregate, and though Boston eventually announced that different schools had different themes, they never put the resources behind them. They just didn't.

"When I think of the future, I have a very pessimistic view. I think that the technology variable is going to make this problem even worse. The affluent will be one group and the people with very little will be in another group. Cities will continue to struggle educationally, and living conditions will continue to deteriorate until maybe we'll have a major social upheaval. Then perhaps the politicians will be willing to put *real* resources into solving the problems.

"What upsets me are these efforts to establish pilot schools and charter schools, because I see them as distractions. They take our focus away from the fact that these problems are very, very complex and very costly. Yet an investment has to be made, and one that a country with six trillion dollar gross national product could easily afford. We don't choose to do it. It's easier for a country, if it doesn't have a good supply of intelligent labor, just to simply ship its factory off shore. It doesn't replace what it does, so there's really no political and economic incentive to improve the lives of poor people who, unfortunately, are usually minority.

"What can be done? Using Boston as my clinical base, I think you have to go back to the fundamentals of recruiting, holding, and developing a strong teacher base. We must get rid of poor teachers, counsel them out of the system, replace them with strong people, use a core of lead teachers who are specially trained who will do nothing but simply work in schools, in classrooms, on a day-to-day basis. We must put good curriculum in place, develop a core of really first-rate principals, and make certain that pedagogical assistance be applied directly in the schools.

"These are the fundamental kinds of things that should happen. And what I see in Boston is a lot of publicity to stuff like charter schools, pilot schools, and the Annenberg program that really is all fluff.

"Boston—and it's true almost everywhere in big cities—has large numbers of people who don't know how to teach and don't particularly care for the kids. And too many of them don't know the subject they are teaching! I would recruit hard for the best and the brightest. If some of our talented college kids knew that this was an honored, important profession, and that they were going to get competitive salaries, strong curriculum, good support systems and working conditions, they could be recruited to work in the schools. But we cannot put these young people into the current urban schools with poor leadership and incompetent colleagues who don't really give a damn in some cases and expect them to survive for a year."

July 7, 1997

Robert (Bud) Spillane

Bud Spillane resigned as superintendent of Fairfax County, Virginia, Public Schools in September 1997. This was his last superintendency, capping a highly successful career as a school superintendent in several districts, including the city of Boston. Now working with the U.S. State Department's overseas schools, he continues to be actively engaged in education.

Spillane has dealt with school desegregation from various settings—suburbs, small cities, New York State Department of Education, large city, and a large urban/suburban county. He grew up in the south end of Hartford, Connecticut, then a predominantly Italian neighborhood, and like most large and small cities of the Northeast, largely isolated from the other ethnic sections of the city.

Indeed, not until he was a college sophomore at the University of Connecticut did he actually confront a racist incident. "I was extremely naïve, and had a good friend, Edward Watson, who still is a very dear friend and formerly a great basketball player. At that time I loved playing basketball and a group of us would occasionally take trips to Boston to watch the Boston Celtics. Our family had moved to Willimantic, Connecticut, and several black families lived there, including my friend, Ed Watson. Well, one day Ed said, 'I have to get a haircut,' and I said 'I do, too. Why don't we go to my barber shop? I go to Lenny's—where do you go?' He kind of fumbled and didn't say much. Then someone grabbed me and said, 'Don't you understand? He has to go to New Haven to get a haircut.' and I said, 'No, no!' And then it hit me. That's how naïve I was as a sophomore in college in 1954.

"Probably my most vivid memory was in Roosevelt, Long Island, just outside New York City and I was a thirty-year-old superintendent in a nearby all-black school district. This was at the time of black militancy. Rody McCoy was living in Roosevelt and leading the Black Panther movement in Ocean Hill/Brownsville, locking horns with Al Shanker (leader of the teachers' union in New York City). McCoy was actually a middle class guy with a lovely wife who played tennis on the weekends after a week of raising hell in Brooklyn. I remember being held hostage for several hours in my office by black militants who resented having a white man as school superintendent.

"When I was in Roosevelt, there wasn't one black administrator, and the faculty was about 10 percent black. So they had good reason for being angry. I appointed all the first black administrators.

"It's interesting that three out of the five members of the school board were black. But they were part of this small city's black middle class who were sharply criticized as being 'Uncle Toms' by the militant blacks like Roy Innis and others from groups like CORE (Congress of Racial Equality). So even in the 1960s, the struggle was being waged among blacks, with militants demanding control over black and segregated schools, and the more moderate blacks of the NAACP and the Urban League pushing for desegregation.

"I remember having several meetings with Betty Shabaz, Malcolm X's widow. At that time, she seemed to be searching for direction regarding race relations, and she talked about Malcolm and what he meant.

"When I got to Boston in 1981, the city had been desegregated by court order for six years. For me, there wasn't any question about desegregation; it was a question of the process, how it was accomplished, and how neighborhoods were selected when busing whites and blacks into angry and hostile neighborhoods. They made the worst choices, busing South Boston kids into Roxbury, the area of the city nearly 100 percent black, and Roxbury kids to South Boston and Charlestown, which were overwhelmingly white and Irish.

"Unlike other cities under court order in California, where they desegregated schools because neighborhoods had changed, in Boston, certain neighborhoods had remained unchanged for generations, and we had to desegregate every year to assure racial balance. Consequently, by 1983, after going through changes the three previous years, we really had a confusing and disturbing situation. Black parents became very upset and would meet with me to express their outrage. The worst case scenario under Judge Garrity's plan was a black family who had five kids in five different elementary schools, and the mother said to me, 'I can't go to five schools. I can't even get into one!'

"As a result of all this busing and school switches, whites were abandoning the city. The racial percentages of the schools in the early 1980s was about 50 percent black and 50 percent white and Asian.

"The judge (W. Arthur Garrity) was totally isolated. I remember meeting him at a reception in Boston shortly after I became superintendent and he asked me where I lived. He was amazed I lived in the city and revealed how out of touch he was with Boston's realities. He had no idea how to integrate and was concerned with winning appeals of his decisions.

"So much of the federal money we received could have been used to strengthen schools, tutor kids, and help close the wide gap in achievement between white and black kids. Instead, it all went into busing. Garrity was truly an obstinate man, and when I was preparing to leave Boston I made a remark about leaving Boston and Judge Garrity's plantation. But I really felt that way, and that he was the master. Well, this was caught by the press, naturally, and it infuriated the judge and the blacks as well. To this day I am reminded of it.

"In spite of our battles with the judge, we still accomplished quite a bit, especially through the 'Boston Compact,' an alliance between the school system and Boston's most prestigious businesses. Our schools were improved, but between the politics of the school committee and racial issues, it was a constant struggle. On top of that, funding was inadequate.

"Exaggerating the hostility displayed by neighborhoods resisting the mixing of blacks and whites, particularly in South Boston and Charlestown, is difficult. Violent acts abounded and included rock throwing and stringing low wires across streets in hopes of knocking policemen off their motorcycles and escaping them. Such acts of violence were not exclusively tied to Boston, since insulated ethnic neighborhoods characterized most cities in the Northeast. But because of the publicity and numerous pictures and accounts of Boston's struggles, the city's reputation as racist was enhanced."

November 5, 1997

Sam Turner

Sam Turner grew up in Newton, Massachusetts, and went through its highly regarded school system. Following high school graduation, he attended the public junior college in this city, which borders Boston. Sam left his home town for Ohio and received his bachelor's degree from Bowling Green University in 1955. Although wanting to return to Massachusetts, he recalls the difficulty he encountered when attempting to get a teaching position in the 1950s.

"I tried to teach in Massachusetts and Connecticut and I kept running up against the old stone wall, segregation and discrimination. But I was offered a teaching position in Canton, Ohio, and gained one year of valuable experience. So I applied again in Newton and this time I was hired to teach in an elementary school along with another black. We became the first two people of color to teach in the Newton Public Schools.

"I taught in Newton for eight years and became interested in becoming a principal. At that time, Chuck Brown was the superintendent and when I spoke with him, he said, "Sam, in order for you to become a principal in Newton, you can't be as good as anyone else. You must be better than any of our white principals.' Well, I saw the handwriting on the wall and realized that there was no chance, at least at that time, to become a principal in Newton.

"During those years I was doing graduate work at Boston University and some of my professors were working with Bill Mahoney, the superintendent of schools in Glastonbury, Connecticut. They were developing new or different schools and were looking for principals interested in leading these programs.

Through this connection I was called to Glastonbury and ended up teaching there for two years. When Mahoney became superintendent in Hingham, Massachusetts, he took me with him, and I continued working with him for two years.

"By now we are into the late 1960s and things were changing. With the assassination of Martin Luther King stimulating the civil rights movement, more opportunities became available in many places, including my native town. Chuck Brown was still the superintendent, and I was asked to come back for an interview. I remember like it was yesterday and can still hear Jim Laurits, the Assistant Superintendent for Personnel, saying, 'You know, Thomas Wolfe wrote a book about not being able to go home again, but I think you can. We need you here, and we know we made some mistakes."

"I was impressed with what Newton was doing, especially with their commitment to staff development and teacher training. That same day, Chuck Brown told me, 'I had the gall, the audacity, to say to you that you had to be better than any white principal. I want you to know that in the last six years I think I have grown a lot, and I now ask for your forgiveness of my ignorance.'

"This led to my being appointed as an administrator, really as a principal and recruiter of African-American teachers—back then we still used the word Negro. I went all over the country looking for minority teachers, particularly throughout the south, and in those years I was very successful because conditions in the south were so poor that young people who finished college probably couldn't get a job, and if they did, it wasn't a very good one. So they were very attracted to the Boston area. I used to bring up carloads of students during spring break, and we had the kind of people who were hiring these folks.

"Jim Laurits said, 'If we can make 10 percent, it would be a critical mass that we can build upon and maintain.' Recruiting became a major assignment for me, and interestingly led me to

Greenville, Mississippi, where I worked with a bunch of principals—all white—who were trying to desegregate, including developing a mixed faculty. These guys were miles apart, trying to do stuff that they were not prepared to do. But I learned a lot from that experience, which helped me when I came back to the Boston area about the time Boston was dealing with *de facto* segregation.

"The METCO program was started and I became involved with that, the Storefront Learning Center, and other projects involving Boston and its suburbs as we attempted to bring blacks and whites together.

"One of the interesting changes in my recruiting efforts is the diminishing number of African-American students who are willing to come to the Boston area for teaching positions. The ground just isn't as fertile any more. There are now 21 school districts in metropolitan Boston trying to bring minority teachers to their schools, but it is no longer as enticing as it used to be. You can live much cheaper in places like Greensboro, North Carolina, Atlanta, Georgia, and Richmond, Virginia. And now there are many more opportunities to teach in the south—plus the fact that there are more opportunities in business and other professions. Competition is unreal! At historically black institutions, there will be 150 recruiters and 60 students.

"Back in the 1960s, principals would say to me, "Sam, if you bring up one of these girls from the south with that accent, the kids won't understand her.' They were constantly looking for reasons not to hire blacks. I remember when I first applied in Newton, I was told my English wasn't good enough. Oh, there were all kinds of ways to slight and insult us. Somehow I bury this stuff in the back of my mind so deep I have a hard time recalling all the instances of discrimination. It would make me very bitter, and I have colleagues and friends who are at that point. They say, 'Sam, how can you do that?' But I find I have to chalk that up to ignorance, and to the fact that people have never had an opportunity to learn to behave differently.

"Remember the days of 'sensitivity training'? And do you recall the programs we had back in the late 60s and early 70s when we took twenty African-American folks who had degrees but not in education? Working with Boston University and Boston State College during summer sessions, we trained these people, gave them certification, and had agreements from school systems in EdCo (Education Collaborative for Greater Boston) to hire them as teachers in their schools. Talk about reinventing the wheel! This is now happening again as a great new idea.

"When you ask me about accomplishments of desegregation, I have some difficulty. It's a hard question. I do feel that one of the things that's been accomplished is the development of awareness of discrimination. People may harbor these prejudices, but they have a sense that it is wrong—especially with younger people who often correct their parents when racial slurs are used.

"I also think there is an awareness of the need to make sure that inner city schools serving black communities must have the same kinds of facilities that other schools in the city enjoy. That kind of discrimination may still exist, but now there is awareness of it.

"One of the things we could have done differently was to involve more people and more agencies at every level in the process of desegregation. Schools were expected to do everything, and we needed a broader coalition of forces—government, community organizations, businesses, *and* schools. At the time, what else could you have done but bus kids?

"I wish we could get a movement back to the cities—people with families. We are witnessing what the Kerner Commission warned us about in 1967, following the riots in Detroit, Los Angeles, Newark, and elsewhere. You know, I see us going back right now, and unfortunately, I think there's a stronger force for that than to move forward. It saddens me because I still think we could push forward and move toward an integrated society that works."

August 20, 1997

(Sam Turner, a former elementary school principal, is now a professor at Leslie College.)

Marty Walsh

From the 20th floor of a downtown office building, Marty Walsh casts his eyes over the city of Boston. This seminarian-trained Catholic priest runs the U.S. Department of Justice Community Relations Office in Boston. He worked closely with Judge Garrity during the tension-filled days of court-ordered school desegregation. He still retains his relationship with Garrity.

Walsh grew up in Pittsburgh, and following his ordination worked in the Miami, Florida, diocese. "I worked on community service and became interested in urban issues and how people were affected by them. In Miami, there was much conflict between blacks and Cubans, and with urbanized farm workers who were being exploited. I helped to organize these workers with assistance from the steel workers of the AFL/CIO. From Florida I went to Washington, D.C., in the mid 1960s and served with the Office of Equal Opportunity under the Johnson Administration. The Justice Department sent me to Boston in 1974 to run the Department's Community Relations Office and I have been here ever since.

"It took little time to feel the anger felt by all the factions involved with school desegregation. By the mid 70s, Boston was close to the edge and violence was at the breaking point. Boston was an anomaly, the only place that went through such a struggle, other than the South, in its opposition to desegregation.

"From 1955 on to the federal court order in 1974, the local government resisted efforts to desegregate. And even though the state passed the racial imbalance law in 1965, it was never enforced. So there were many guilty parties, and this resistance led to federal involvement.

"The opportunities to make changes, take actions, were missed. Probably the Boston School Committee deserves the most blame, but the politics of the city, from the mayor's office to the neighborhood precincts, were in denial. There was no effort to do anything other than to obfuscate or obstruct any attempt to comply with the law.

"Year One of the desegregation plan was such a failure! All it accomplished was to move students around the city—really just a busing program. How they (the State Department of Education) decided to move kids from Roxbury into South Boston and Charlestown just baffles me. The most solidly imbedded black and Irish neighborhoods fought to protect their home turfs as most expected them to do. And Judge Garrity gave them opportunity to prepare for the changes necessary to comply with the law. The city did nothing to plan for desegregation.

"In 1974, then Superintendent Leary complained that the School Committee wouldn't let him do anything. Bill Leary also wanted to be reappointed by the five-member, hardnosed committee headed at that time by John Kerrigan, who had succeeded Louise Day Hicks. Both of these people were notorious in their opposition to desegregate the schools. I don't think there was a mean bone in Leary's body, but he grew up in Boston, taught in the schools, and didn't buck the system. He was always in a dilemma, and adjusted to the system and the political machine.

"When the 'shit hit the fan,' the mayor, Kevin White, took the rap. At the time, it seemed close to anarchy, yet there was no coordinated plan to deal with the crisis. White essentially said that it is the federal government's responsibility, and this was a mayor who had national ambitions, including a desire to run for president. He will tell you to this day that busing and the struggle over school desegregation ruined the dreams he had for higher office.

"Despite all the criticism and the enduring negative impression of Boston's desegregation efforts, all the illegal policies that had taken place in Boston were eliminated. And that's all, basically, the judge could do. He tried to do more, and he did as much as he could. At least he set in motion what had to be done, with very little, if any, help from the school system.

"Prior to Judge Garrity, a principal in Boston would often be responsible for two, sometimes three schools. Buildings and resources had been neglected for years, and there was no constituency of any consequence for the public schools in Boston. More than 70 percent of the families of public school kids were on welfare. Poor children were the majority in the public schools and here, at least, there was no discrimination. These kids were from both white and black families.

"The judge brought in more resources and money to Boston. He tried to involve people to assist in desegregation, and did succeed in a limited way. Individuals like Tracy Amalfitano, Jim Sullivan, Peter Cooney, and others put themselves on the line and were heroic.

"In the 1970s, Boston schools were living in the past and were out-of-date. For example, when I would ask for attendance figures, officials would look at file cards, for God's sake! That's how they kept track of things. Claims would be made that there were 93,000 kids in the school system prior to desegregation. When we got involved, there was no centralized way of checking the numbers. Principals would call in and provide figures of their own making. Computers were lacking and no reliable accounting of students existed. Of course, these school counts determined how many teachers and resources each school would have.

"When outside administrators were hired, like Bob Wood (former chancellor of the University of Massachusetts) and Bud Spillane (who came from the State of New York where he had been Deputy State School Superintendent), some changes resulted. Both of these superintendents wanted Judge Garrity to bow out so they could run the schools without court oversight.

"Being closely watched by the court was opposed, understandably. But the judge didn't run the schools—the rules did.

"Judging Boston's schools is unfair, because they are usually compared with the suburban schools—like comparing apples with oranges. They never seem to compare Boston with its urban counterparts, and people forget, or pay no attention to the environments the kids come from.

"I think Boston is moving toward more segregated schools, a dilemma facing a lot of cities. But our only hope is to have an integrated society. I believe we are making progress. The churches are working more collaboratively, and blacks and whites are meeting to resolve problems. We have lacked leadership, and we need leaders to put these matters on the front burner. There are a number of positive things happening, and progress never moves in a straight line. More black kids are graduating and going on to college. I think there has been progress."

August 25, 1998

Bob Watson

In 1965, the Massachusetts State Department of Education published "Because It Is Right—Educationally: Report of the Advisory Committee on Racial Imbalance and Education." Soon after, Bob Watson was hired and given major responsibility to respond to the recommendations of the report, one of the sources that led to desegregation of Boston's public schools.

Bob Watson is a flexible bureaucrat, intelligent and with vision to recognize how good ideas can be backed by government funding with relative ease, making possible some programs that have proved to be lasting and influential. For example, under Title III of Congress's original Elementary and Secondary Education Act, Watson recognized those programs and proposals that had creativity combined with an awareness of realities. Consequently, an innovative program like the Education Collaborative for Greater Boston (EdCo) was formed in 1968 and still serves Boston and its suburbs. (Title III encouraged and funded such proposals.)

Designed to develop programs that tied Boston with seven metropolitan suburbs in several collaborative programs, it now includes more than twenty school districts. It had the potential to be a much more significant metropolitan model until the Supreme Court in the Milligan II case struck down a metropolitan plan that included the city of Detroit and surrounding Michigan suburbs in 1977.

Watson: "In the late 1960s and 70s, we were fighting each other within the department (Massachusetts Department of Education). While some of us were struggling to support desegregation and innovative programs, others, largely in the business department, opposed these programs. And in some cases they were correct, because they were 'loosey-goosey' plans, especially financially.

"In those years, several key people were willing to take risks and believed in desegregation—people like Bob Sperber, Chuck Brown, Jim Laurits, Aaron Fink, and Rudy Fobert were suburban superintendents actively involved. Black leadership at that time was very strong and leaders were very patient and understanding. Ruth Batson, Jean McGuire, and Ellen Jackson come to mind.

"On the other hand, many people in the Boston school bureaucracy and city government were not the least bit interested in desegregation and would do anything to undermine efforts—particularly the School Committee. They were not only not constructive but destructive.

"I think desegregation helped a lot of kids. Look, segregation in any form is bad. It separates us and has caused great problems for this country, throughout our history. And there's no question that public schools have made significant contributions in bringing together diverse groups, not only racially and ethnically but also religiously and economically. So now the popular view is that conservatives are attacking public schools and advocating vouchers for private and parochial schools. Well, my view of being conservative is to preserve those traditions and institutions that have made this country great.

"Desegregation has also raised the awareness of a lot of adults. Garrity (Judge Garrity) was a very courageous judge and his court order pinpointed many really egregious things that were going on. If you change a law and people have to abide by the law, that's good. It's hard to legislate morality or attitudes, but maybe their children and the children of their children will have changed from the views of parents who supported segregation. Some behaviors have absolutely changed and opportunities have opened up, but we have a long way to go.

"As to where we may be headed, I am a short-term pessimist and a long-term optimist. I think things will evolve and we will get things out of our system. For example, I am not enamored with charter schools. They really are a cop-out to supporting the public system. Are the poor families going to be able to transport their children? To say 'We shall allow parents to choose any school in the state,' as Governor Weld recently proclaimed, is to pander to the worst instincts in some people.

"I am always hopeful. If you want a good school, you must have good teachers. And we need leaders to stimulate us, and who have the courage to support a national movement to improve public schools. I support the military model, like the Naval Academy or West Point. If we had a program that paid full tuition to our finest colleges for four years in return for four years of public service in our urban public schools, that would have a powerful and positive effect."

August 26, 1997

(Bob Watson was formerly the Superintendent of Schools in Sommerville, Massachusetts.)

Kevin White

The office that Kevin White enjoys now is hardly a comedown from the grandeur of the accommodations afforded him when he served as mayor. His new office in a renovated Boston townhouse overlooks the Charles River on Boston University's urban campus. It reflects White's style and taste for Brahmin elegance. He may no longer have the political power provided Boston's mayors, but his appreciation of it is transferred to his new role as one of the university's most popular professors. His classes are regularly over-subscribed. His experience, knowledge, and inherent charm make this most understandable.

The four consecutive terms he served provided White abundant background to teach both the theoretical and pragmatic components of politics. So prominent was he at one stage of his career, he was within a hair's breadth of being on the Democratic ticket as vice president when George McGovern ran against Richard Nixon in the election of 1972. This episode really whetted White's appetite for national office, and he became seriously interested in running for the presidency in 1976.

But being mayor of Boston during the turbulent years when Judge Garrity ordered Boston to desegregate its public schools became overwhelming. It damaged severely his chances for higher office. Now enjoying teaching and with the years of being mayor behind him, Kevin White is more mellow and reflective in recalling those exceptionally tense times.

"Anthony Lukas wrote quite a chapter on me in his book, *Common Ground*. Yes, it was beautifully written and deserving of a Pulitzer Prize. But it was a little too personal for me, especially when he described the relationship between my father and me. And some other details were not that accurate, but all in all, Lukas was pretty close to the mark. I am a fathead, but not that much of a fathead!

"Busing tore up Boston, not really the issue of desegregation. And it is rare to have an entire city have what I call a nervous breakdown. For me, who at that time had aspirations for higher political office, it was a nightmare. In looking back, perhaps I was a bit pretentious, and I had some dreams.

"For all the turmoil and the rampant emotions, there were no murders, no hangings, no white sheets, or anything like that. It was an emotional screaming contest stimulated by fear more than anger. Detroit was entirely different—that was anger, a three-day anger! Boston wasn't like Los Angeles or New York, and certainly not like Selma. You could feel hatred in other places involved with civil rights issues. Here it was fear. There's a difference between hatred and being terrorized—entirely different. Southie (South Boston, a section of Boston nearly solidly Irish) was terrorized and threatened.

"At the time, I was mentally leaving town. I was 'traveling'—off in a world by myself. You must understand that the mayor of Boston is all-powerful, more than any other city I know, and 99 percent of the Celtic people wanted and expected me to be on their side. Back in 1974, once I knew Mondale and Teddy (Walter Mondale and Ted Kennedy) were politically dead, I saw opportunity. Five seconds with Carter (Jimmy Carter, who got the Democratic presidential nomination in 1976) and I said to myself, 'This is lunchtime!' I thought I could beat him, and at that time I felt a calm, good confidence. And busing ended it. I knew it was over! (White had reason to express these feelings, because he *was* riding high politically before the explosive issue of desegregating schools hit Boston.)

"When you mention Louise Day Hicks, who became immersed in the issue of school busing, I have to say she was over her head and didn't understand it. Oh sure, she rode the hell out of the issue, but it got out of control. She really wasn't a hater; she was frightened and saw political opportunity for herself. She became a national symbol for racial hatred. If she looked like Grace Kelly, she would have been treated better. She and John Kerrigan (both chaired the Boston School Committee) did all they could to delay and prevent school desegregation. Kerrigan was a bad guy and didn't care about anyone. He was so crude, and the only person in the city who would thumb his nose at the two most powerful forces in the city—the cardinal and *The Boston Globe*.

"When it comes to leadership in the black community, the one who had the most quality and respect was Mrs. Cass (longtime African-American activist, no longer alive). I remember one community meeting with much shouting and with emotions running high, and Mrs. Cass told the crowd to shut up so Louise Day Hicks could speak. She had so much respect in the black community that the crowd quieted down, and Hicks was allowed to speak.

"The problem was to find spokesmen to speak for the blacks who had influence. I could communicate with the white 'pols' but I couldn't reach black leadership. I was OK with blacks generally, but not the leadership. In fairness, they were right to give up on the school system. The school bureaucracy felt it was their system and schools were just fine. Only Arthur Gartland, a liberal on the school committee who was not a politician, sensed that change was coming.

"What went wrong? The issue (desegregation) in Boston was addressed fundamentally as a serious problem in education when it was actually a *political* problem. You cannot tell an educator about the nuances of politics, particularly in the middle of a war. And you cannot tell 'pols' about the needs of education when their careers are threatened. The approach used was the wrong prescription for the patient. It was not pragmatic and became a political disaster.

"Garrity (Judge Arthur W. Garrity of the federal court who ordered the desegregation plan) angered me terribly. I lost my temper in his court house. I walked out. And I should never have gone down to the courthouse in the first place. I didn't have to go. It was just frustration. I'm all Irish and I lost it! Garrity is the epitome of obstinacy and insularity. He was just the wrong man at the wrong time. He couldn't understand the passion, didn't know Boston, lived in the wealthy suburb of Wellesley—a lace-curtain Irishman. Here was a man who had it within his power to resolve the problem. With one stroke, he could have resolved it without surrendering. It was just like an O'Neill play!

"Integration is more acceptable in good times, and in those years we had the heavy hitters in place. The Kennedys, Margaret Chase Smith (former senator from Maine). They were there (political leaders), and economically, New England was doing well. We still had the high tech industry with us, but it is highly mobile.

"The only way to address this problem of school desegregation is through public policy and the political process. In Massachusetts, unlike other states, the Mayor of Boston, the Speaker of the House in the state, the President of the State Senate, and the Governor have tremendous political power. They can do whatever they want. You can have a Speaker of the House who is a roaring idiot and he can do what he wants because he runs the House! Enormous power! Collectively, these four individuals could create a metropolitan plan for schools and implement it."

April 24, 1998

Charles Willie

Chuck Willie is a professor of education at Harvard. Now in his 22nd year at the Graduate School of Education, he is sensing a form of regression regarding desegregation. His journey through life provides remarkable insights to the story of school desegregation. As an African-American born and raised in the deep south, he *lived* segregation, going to all-black public schools and graduating from Morehouse College in Atlanta, Georgia.

Willie came to Harvard in 1974 and has been actively involved with Boston's schools and desegregation plans. His demeanor is friendly and casual as he reflects upon his experiences in his little office that is overflowing with books and papers.

"I'm worried about a 'closing down' in a society that should be open. As we struggle with race issues, there is also a growing movement to establish English as our official language. It reminds me of the wave of anti-immigrant sentiment in the 1920s when we had a chance to be a multilingual nation and lost it. English will prevail without the need to establish it as our official language. I'm very much against the one-language advocates. To be a great nation we must be inclusive. And this relates to the cause of desegregation. My fear is the fractionalization of our schools.

"While we move closer to a half century since the Brown decision that overthrew the doctrine of 'separate but equal,' the current trend to return to separateness is very disturbing. I understand it. Many blacks have been disillusioned and feel betrayed, especially those who took huge risks. Still it was important to require white schools to desegregate, even though it meant much greater disruption to black families.

"We tend to overlook the accomplishments of desegregation—and they *are* extraordinary! It woke up whites! Earlier, many whites believed the Constitution should be obeyed only if it was beneficial to them. Take Virginia, for example. Even Virginia, with its ties to Jefferson, Washington, and Madison! Can you imagine the state governor closing all the public schools! And finally, he had to open all of those schools. For the first time, a governor who had to swear to obey the law of the land tried to disobey it, and he couldn't get away with it.

"It was important to prove we are a nation of laws. Actually, I have maintained that even if *Plessy vs. Ferguson* had been upheld by the Supreme Court in 1954, we still would have ended school segregation because it would have been too expensive. States never came close to obeying the law (establishing separate but equal) prior to 1954. They could not afford it and got away with violating the law even before the Brown decision. Nobody made them obey the law. School desegregation saved this nation as a constitutional democracy. It helped *everybody* understand that they had to obey the law. Think about it. Equipment and facilities had to be upgraded. Linguistic minorities had to be accommodated. Schools did not have to do this before. Children with special needs had to be admitted to schools. Prior to school desegregation, at least one-third of special-needs youngsters were not accepted in public schools. Then the final thing that happened was with women who had been shortchanged for years. Now (he chuckles) women have to be admitted to military schools. All these massive changes are due to school desegregation. I can go on. The whole magnet-school movement that has helped to reform schools while providing options came right out of school desegregation. And ironically, it was beneficial to whites if one thinks of the Baake case (reverse discrimination case at the University of California).

"The requirement of diversity has been beneficial to all of us. My plan in Boston, going back to 1989, is controlled choice.

Every person has access to any school in a zone. There are roughly twenty schools in each zone, but you could only go to an unassigned school if you were in the racial proportion of the zone or if the established racial balance was not affected. Ninety percent of the students and families are getting what they want. Let each group have its own culture but share it with others.

"Oh yes, mistakes were made! For example, in most cases there was no group assigned to monitor the process. A well-developed, organized plan was lacking. School districts may have thought they had a plan—indeed they did have plans—but the commitment necessitating careful monitoring and implementation wasn't there. Another mistake—in hindsight—was the courts assigning the task of desegregation to local school boards, most of whom were either resisting or reluctant about desegregating schools in the first place. A third mistake was to attain professional assistance (consulting) from white males. Whoever was used for outside assistance needed to be 'in line' or sensitive to the blacks and their concerns. Many desegregation plans were most offensive to blacks and least offensive to whites. In Milwaukee, for example, black kids were bused nine-to-one over whites."

Part III
Louisville

In June 1989, the Kentucky Supreme Court issued an opinion that held the system of common schools in Kentucky to be unconstitutional. This significant decision covered the entire gamut of the common school system in Kentucky and placed upon the General Assembly the responsibility of recreating and re-establishing a new system of common schools throughout the state.

Following an intensive year of study with task forces working on curriculum, governance, and finance, the Kentucky Education Reform Act (KERA) emerged. It became law on July 13, 1990. Affecting all school systems throughout the Commonwealth of Kentucky, it plays an interesting and significant role within the Jefferson County schools.

Nowhere in KERA is race mentioned. It certainly is implied through the orders of the Supreme Court of Kentucky, which requires that all common schools be free to all, that they be substantially uniform throughout the state and provide equal educational opportunities to all Kentucky children. There are many other broad stipulations listed in the Court's statement, but desegregation or race as an issue is unmentioned. There is little doubt that conflict will develop between Jefferson County schools and the KERA requirements.

Enrollment figures and racial percentages taken as a whole show a stability that is encouraging. When birthrate statistics for Jefferson County are reviewed, it shows an increasing percentage of African-American births over the last two decades and the reverse trend for whites. For the school district, the racial balance has been 70 percent white and 30 percent black for the past decade. The fact that it has remained constant (30.7 percent) demonstrates a holding power that is remarkably different from other urban school systems.

In 1994, 34 elementary schools had a racial balance ranging from 23 to 43 percent black. Twenty-five elementary schools had less than 23 percent African-American children, with the range descending from 22 to 16 percent. Twenty-three elementary schools had more than 43 percent African-American children, with a descending range from 50 to 44 percent.

Elementary clusters had roughly six or seven schools in each cluster. Figures revealing racial enrollment for the 13 clusters in 1994 were:

- Four clusters had more African-American children than in 1991.
- Five clusters had fewer African-American children than in 1991.
- Four clusters remained the same.

Put another way:

- Four clusters had fewer white children than in 1991.
- Five clusters had more white children than in 1991.
- Four clusters remained the same.

Middle schools kept within the new guidelines with African-American percentages running from 22.6 percent to 44.2

percent, or an average of 31 percent. With the exception of Central, only Western High School at 42 percent and Shawnee at 41 percent had percentages above 40. The average African-American student population in Jefferson County high schools was about 35 percent. For a school district committed to desegregation these are positive numbers.

Total student enrollment since 1984 has remained stable. Since 1991, enrollment increased slightly, from 91,693 to 92,786 in September 1993; September 1994 numbers were essentially the same at 92,747. More than 5,000 were in the Early Childhood Program.

Schools appear to be especially important to people in Jefferson County, Kentucky. Not that they are unimportant elsewhere, but in my visits to Louisville, and based upon wide experience covering many years with schools and communities, I see that the Jefferson County Public Schools are a major concern. Certainly the main newspaper, the *Courier Journal*, contributes largely to this interest in schools. Education and schools are of great interest to the managing editor, David Hawpe.

Essential to an evaluation of the 1993 desegregation plan are the reactions of individuals and groups.

Five representatives of QUEST (Quality Education for All Students) met with me on June 20, 1994. Although many of the same views expressed by members of the Monitoring Committee were repeated, other comments added to the community's concerns with regard to desegregation. This group agreed that a noticeable change had occurred in the administration from the concentrated effort made in 1975 to accomplish desegregation. This change refers primarily to the previous superintendent, Donald Ingwerson, but also included central administration in general. These QUEST representatives felt that there was less emphasis on making desegregating work and more emphasis on elite approaches such as tracking through the advanced program plus one-way busing.

There was also a sense that some manipulation took place before the approval of the latest desegregation plan. Some believed that the law firm hired by the Board deliberately selected individuals from the African-American community who agreed with the Board's new plan. The implication expressed was that some key leaders in the community, including leading businessmen working with the administration, developed a plan and succeeded in having it approved by the Board without sufficient community involvement. QUEST representatives did not see busing as the main problem but attributed tracking and general inequity as being the main deficiencies of the new desegregation plan.

There was still belief among these representatives that some clusters had become stronger. It was suggested that the school system develop policies on how the clusters would accomplish the best of the plan.

Many individuals outside the school system who had active involvement with the Jefferson County schools remained very much interested in what happened. One of the most interesting of these interviews was with a legend in Louisville, Lyman Johnson. This retired teacher, administrator, and civil rights activist had a grasp on history, in particular civil rights, that made him a special resource. This eighty-eight-year-old gentleman—a scholar who spent forty years in the school system—was discouraged about what was happening in the neighborhood, the nation, and the world.

On May 23, 1994, he said "I think the magnet idea has about run its course and I'm not sure where we're going but I'm also afraid of where we may go." He felt that Project Renaissance was doomed to failure. He said, "Once you are segregated, you have lost it. Your chances are much more limited and you continue to swim in shallow water."

Johnson also recognized that mandatory busing was expensive and very cumbersome. But the end of our interview was somewhat encouraging as Lyman Johnson expressed the hope that the day would come when mixed neighborhoods would result in schools that are naturally desegregated.

Lucien Gates, III

Assistant Superintendent for Secondary Schools and Formerly Principal of Western High School

We need to examine the message we send students. Are we saying that you are poor, unwashed, unmanageable, or are we sending the message that you are capable, able, and worthy? We must teach and show our children that we can be responsible for each other and that we care about each other and that we can help each other. We can show them that school is a place to gain knowledge, a place to become successful, and most of all a place of high expectations that send the message "this is important," "you can do it," and "I will not give up on you."

We have a corporation that has said "I'm going to put my money where my mouth is. I'm going to give you the money and the resources to make it work." I have a faculty and a staff who tirelessly give of themselves to ensure students' success.

But I need some parents. I need some parents who will insist that their child is in school on a daily basis, and on time.

I need some parents who insist that students' homework is done daily.

I need some parents who insist that students take responsibility for their own actions or their inaction, however the case may be.

I need some parents who will insist that students are healthy and free from chemical or drug abuse.

Rev. Louis Coleman
Pastor, Shelby Congregational Methodist Church, Shelbyville

... The problem with the Jefferson County School System continues to be the lack of black teachers hired by the system. At this date the system has an 800 black-teacher gap; a total of 853 black teachers are in the system today. Before desegregation, the Louisville system had over 1,000 black teachers in the system. Upon desegregation and merger, the black teachers were phased out and literally pushed out of the system. But the system has never recouped and regained these teachers for several reasons—lack of an aggressive recruiting team, teachers within the system who felt that the system was not salable; lack of aggressiveness by those staff members who have been given the charge to recruit.

If the system can make an about-face in desegregation and integrating its coaching staff in less than a year's time in major sports, it certainly can do the same with its teacher core.

Claudia Runge
Seventh-Grade Language Arts Teacher at Kammerer Middle School

This year marks my 22nd year of teaching and my 20th year teaching in Jefferson County Public Schools. For 18 years I've taught advanced program classes and regular program classes in the seventh grade.

As a teacher and parent, I am concerned about the tracking of middle school students. I definitely think that students' civil rights are being violated and that middle schools are not truly integrated under this system. I am convinced that academic achievement is inhibited under the tracking system. Finally, the social and emotional growth of middle school children is stunted when they are segregated and labeled by the academic track in which they are placed.

Black children are woefully under-represented in advanced program classes. The situation in honors classes is not much better.

Research says that accurate placement is difficult if not impossible. Furthermore, achievement is not increased. Maybe the top 10 percent achieve more, but the bottom 90 percent achieve less in tracking situations.

In most of our middle schools, the students in one class stay together all day long with the same friends, who provide few if any positive role models for one another. Students internalize failure, and this gets worse as each year passes. Unfortunately, this is especially a problem for black children because they are over-represented in regular program classes.

They can't and don't learn to understand and get along with people of other races, cultures, income levels, neighborhoods, and abilities.

Children in all three tracks suffer emotionally and socially from ability grouping; however, black children bear the brunt of this problem. The "regular program" label that most of them wear translates to low self-esteem, not exactly the best ingredient for healthy social and emotional growth.

Carmen Weathers
Parent and Teacher

I'm here because I'm an African-American. I'm here because I'm a public school teacher. I'm here because I'm a citizen of these United States. I'm here because I'm a concerned parent. I think I have something that needs to be said.

Education is the one humanizing force that we, as American citizens, are all entitled to by law.

If any segment of your school population is denied that humanizing and civilizing agent and impact that education can bring to us by default, it is not doing its job. If it in any sense robs me of my potential as a human being, if it denies who I am, if it calls into question my genetic superiority or inferiority, it is, by law, wrong.

The first thing that an education ought to do is tell me who I am. It ought to let me look at myself and reflect me through the world that I live in. If that educational system does not do that, it is not educating me; it is programming me to take some jobs. I don't want black children to have jobs; I want them to create jobs.

Beverly Moore
Parent Activist

I'm going to speak to you from my experience as a parent. I now have two children in Jefferson County Schools. My youngest son is in a school where the counselor assured me that advanced program and non-advanced program students were all treated just the same.

He said, "Mom, they don't put black kids in AP classes." The twelve-year-old knew exactly what was happening in his school.

My daughter's friend said that she doesn't even have the opportunity to meet black students because of the segregation within the school.

My daughter reports that the students are still separated and there's still hostility between the groups. She doesn't know any of them well enough to understand their feelings.

Why is this segregation tolerated in Jefferson County schools? The segregation is caused by the tracking of students, as you've heard, and to AP, honors, regular, special ed, and magnet classes. Tracking does not increase achievement and has negative effects.

Tracking is used to attract upper middle class parents to the public schools by providing the equivalent of an exclusive private school within the public schools. This has resulted in the segregation of the students and the inherently unequal education that accompanies it.

For example, there is a math program called Simal that in Jefferson County is used exclusively with AP classes. Ironically, it is not a program designed for gifted or advanced students but for the whole range of abilities. I have been requesting its use with all kids, but the response is always that it must be reserved for the AP program so that they will have a special curriculum. The need of the other students to learn conceptual math is apparently not a consideration.

At a recent open house, parents of AP and non-AP children on the same middle school team were listening to the English teacher's presentation. She explained that some students were using "Word Clues" because those students would be taking the SAT later. Parents of non-AP students were surprised. They didn't know that the school had already decided which students would be taking the SAT or that their children were not being prepared for it, as the other students were.

When the students from this team take the SAT in high school, those who have been in the AP classes, none of whom are black, will probably do better in vocabulary and in math comprehension than the black and white kids from the same team who are in the lower-level classes. The assumption will be that those kids are smarter or had a better home background or that they tried harder. The fact that the other kids never had an opportunity to learn "Word Clues" or to be taught Simal math will not be mentioned. The perception that poor kids and black kids are not as capable will be preserved so that it will justify the continued segregation of those children.

Robert Douglas

Associate Professor at the University of Louisville, Chair of the Pan-African Studies Department

I have firsthand knowledge of the failure of the Jefferson County Public School System to implement a multicultural, multiethnic learning experience for its students, especially as it relates to African Americans' experience.

Most of the African-American students coming to U. of L. from JCPS have little or no awareness or appreciation of the immense contributions that people of African descent have given to the world and the United States.

The inequity of the number of nonwhite students being reprimanded and suspended also speaks to the failure of our society. Thus the Jefferson County Public School System can implement regulations that ensure that its educators have a basic understanding of its African-American students as well as other students of a non-European background. Only then can it begin to give the kind of information to the students to ensure that such racist practices and attitudes do not continue.

Joseph H. McMillan

Professor, Department of Early Childhood Development, University of Louisville

Kentucky has a tremendous opportunity to reform its entire public school system. This local community has a great challenge that it faces.

In a large urban school district like Louisville, Jefferson County, it is imperative that required courses in African-American history and culture be offered.

Secondly, I recommend that our school system adopt as an over-arching goal the motto "All children can learn."

Thirdly, I recommend that our school system focus on developing the thinking and problem-solving skills of its students.

Fourthly, I recommend that our school system design staff development programs to systematically deal with racism and sexism.

And finally, I recommend that our school system and its employees raise their level of expectation for all children.

I agree with government and school officials who state that Kentucky has a golden opportunity to lead this nation in education reform.

Part IV
Alexandria

Directly across the Potomac River from Washington, D.C., is the city of Alexandria, Virginia. It is a densely populated city of about 130,000 people living within 15 square miles.

Remarkable changes have occurred since the mid-60s. In 1954, Alexandria was a completely segregated city beginning to change from a sleepy southern city to a more cosmopolitan urban community. Government workers, employees of corporations receiving government contracts, lawyers and lobbyists were settling in, coming from all over the country, particularly from the Midwest. It is interesting to note that in 2001, the two candidates for mayor were both African-American men.

When the 1954 Brown decision became law, Alexandria joined the massive resistance movement supported by Virginia and other southern states. T. C. Williams, the Superintendent of Schools, did all he could to thwart the desegregation ruling. It is so ironic that the current T. C. Williams High School, named for the former segregationist superintendent, is now a school for students from all over the world, many of them refugees from war-tossed countries, going to classes with whites and the predominate African-American students. Students speak at least thirty languages. T. C. Williams High School has become one of the most exciting high schools in the country. It was named one of the nation's most outstanding high schools and representatives received this award in a ceremony held in the Rose Garden of the White House in 1985. Secretary of Education Terrence Bell presented the award.

Quite likely what brought most attention to Alexandria schools, particularly to T. C. Williams High School, was the popular film, *Remember the Titans,* starring actor Denzel Washington. Like most movies that depict historic events, the film contains some inaccuracies and a bit of hyperbole. However, the essential story of how Alexandria made dramatic changes to desegregate its schools is factual.

In the mid-1960s, John C. Albohm became the city's new Superintendent of Schools, coming from New York State. He worked with federal officials to desegregate the schools and they were declared in compliance in 1966.

Tim Elliott

Interviewed on July 11, 2006

Tim Elliott, former chair of the Alexandria School Board, is retired from his position as deputy associate solicitor for the Department of Commerce but remains active in various civic activities.

Tell me about your early beginnings, where you were born, and how you wound up in Alexandria.

I was born in New York City in 1938. About six or eight months later my parents moved to Alexandria, Virginia. My father worked for the U.S. government. During the war we moved back to New York City. I was in kindergarten and first grade. In second grade we moved back to Virginia. My father, having been raised in New York City, believed that if you could see a house from your house, you had to move. We moved to Burke, Virginia. Someone built a house across the street so we moved to Herndon.

When I went off to college, my father left the government and went to work in California. I attended college and law school in Boston. I went to Brandeis University for college and then went to Harvard Law School. Because I was raised in Northern Virginia, I wanted to live here so I told IBM that if they had a job for a new lawyer in Washington I'd like to have it. They hired me. I've lived in Alexandria since 1964 except for one year when I worked for IBM in Connecticut and Armonk, New York.

How would you describe the reaction to the Brown decision in Virginia towns and Alexandria specifically?

Remember, I was in high school, in Fairfax High School in Fairfax County. When we left New York and came back to Virginia from mid-second grade through high school I was always in a segregated school. I had gone to kindergarten and first grade in the heart of Manhattan and those schools were integrated schools so I went to school with black children. When we came down here, I didn't think too much about it. I did understand about the Brown vs. Board of Education decision in 1954. I called up a conservative friend of ours, who was backing the Gray Plan, a plan to keep Virginia schools segregated. And they did do so. I called up a friend of my parents and she was an adult and I said, "This is outrageous, they will keep the schools segregated." It was called massive resistance. She hung up on me.

They closed the schools in Prince Edward County and set up private academies to maintain segregation, schools for whites only. Starting private academies was done in lots of places in Virginia. In Fairfax County and the rest of Northern Virginia, that was unusual. Northern Virginia is still unusual today compared to other parts of the state.

Up through my ninth-grade year, there were only four high schools in Fairfax County. My graduating class was 140 students, about half of them children of farmers and local people who worked in gas stations and such. The other half were probably children of civil servants or military families. The local children seemed to be adamant about maintaining segregation. They felt that if you let blacks into the schools the quality of education would go down.

Black children in Fairfax County had to go either to Manassas or to Alexandria for high school. Alexandria had Parker Gray. There was no black high school in Fairfax County but they built one. It's maybe a middle school now. One rumor at the white high schools was that Luther Jackson, the new high school for blacks, had a swimming pool. None of our schools had a pool so there were those who said, "Can I go there?"

It was unusual for me. We lived in Burke and Herndon from 1949 to 1959. In both those places we had a black family in our proximity. Each had a son about my age and we were very good friends, but only after school or on weekends. We rode bikes together and played ball together. We would pal around. Later, in 1976, I ran into one of those friends who was in the same basic training unit with me in the Army at Fort Dix. His brother had actually gotten a scholarship to play basketball at Ohio State. He'd never gone to college. I think he went to Osborne High School in Manassas.

There were those who thought (outside of Virginia) that later on there would be busing. But remember, Virginia stayed segregated. The white people closed Prince Edward County schools and started private academies. The word academy became a bad word because it meant this was a segregated white school started to avoid desegregation.

The legislature was behind it, Mr. Gray and the governor were segregationists and wanted to maintain segregation. That's the way things were. I was not an activist at that time; I tried to look at the issue dispassionately. I remember that the statistics were one black student for every twenty-six white students in Fairfax County. I wondered "What are people afraid of in terms of deterioration of education? Let's assume they are correct. Four percent won't do much." That was the attitude. We had always gone to segregated schools when I lived in Virginia.

When our kids began school in Alexandria—our daughter was born in 1965 and our son in 1967—the schools were integrated, but it was not necessarily a healthy integration. That got changed, particularly in the elementary schools.

Who would you say in schools you attended or in communities where you lived did the most they could to prevent desegregation?

I can't remember the name of the Fairfax County superintendent at the time—my guess is that he and the school board had just built a brand new black high school, so the conventional attitude was "They (blacks) have a new school, so why do they want to go to school with our kids?" There was a true belief in separate but equal. Indeed, at a later time, we found out that the education of teachers in black schools was probably superior on balance to those who taught white kids.

How about the other side of the coin? Who was most influential in helping break down the barriers to desegregation?

I suspect, but I don't know for sure, that when I left high school, we still had segregation. I went off to college in 1956 and didn't return here till 1964. By then the artificial barriers the state had created were breaking down, particularly in Northern Virginia. One of the most instrumental things that happened was that Arlington County petitioned the state legislature to let them have an elected school board.

Those were the days of Armistead Boothe, a relative liberal, and Howard Smith and Harry Byrd, and the general wisdom was that the Byrd organization had control of the state through the court houses in those 100 counties that we had. But Arlington was always an anomaly. They got permission for an elected school board, then the elected school board decided to integrate the schools. The legislature said "Wait a minute, we didn't mean for you to have an elected school board so you could integrate the schools, thereafter no more elected school board!"

I think influential was that Arlington County did it for a little while. But desegregation in Arlington schools was no great problem. Arlington County kids were the children of military and civil service families and they were more liberal on that issue because they had lived in other places and had experienced integration themselves. So I think it was predominantly the new students were the children of parents who had moved into the area and had no unreasonable fear about integration.

On the other side, many feared that integration and socialization with blacks would be the end of civilization as they knew it. They feared socializing with blacks. They worried about their daughter dating a black man. Many fears were raised up. Of course it hasn't been. In fact, it has been better for civilization probably.

Focus now on Alexandria and about the city of Alexandria, the hiring, a little about T.C. Williams and the move from Williams to Albohm.

T.C. Williams was of the old school, John Albohm was a fresh voice. He saw that the wave of the future was not adherence to the past necessarily. Our kids walked to Lyles-Crouch. Parents in our neighborhood were of different minds. One mind was if the kids got to the fourth grade, the quality of education went down because kids were starting to grow up, and they were interested in other things, and they got more aggressive. A lot of parents said we need to maintain our public school system and make sure it's a quality system and let's work for that. Some took their children out and sent them to private schools.

That "Old Town" group was so important in keeping middle class whites.

They did for a long time but when the schools were paired to get racial balance, also to avoid being taken over by the federal courts, my mother (who lived in California) said "It's horrible that your children have to be bused." I said they are bused two miles. We said, "When I went to high school I had to change buses, for heaven's sake" We said we think it's good for the system and good for the children. We want diversity—and that meant black and white. We didn't have many Hispanics then. I thought it was a good thing. We were living in Connecticut when they did the real pairing and T.C. became only grades 11 and 12. I guess that created problems, mostly among the white community. Maybe the blacks were upset because it meant some of their teachers would not be teaching their children and that their children were going to get a different challenge than in the past. I remember when I was on the school board, one member said he went to high school in D.C. because he was going to go to college and you didn't go to Parker Gray.

So the changeover was a refreshing wind that blows and you know it's going to bring change and good weather with Albohm. Mr. Williams was tied to the past, as was the superintendent of Fairfax County when I was there.

I remember when I came here and we would go to sporting events. Betty got a kick out of it because of the mystique of T.C. Williams. The shouting of "TC, TC," scared the hell out of the other kids. Now there has been such a change. Fairfax County schools are so remarkably changed and integrated now.

That's been a good thing, too. Bob, because when we returned here, the black middle class didn't want to live in Northern Virginia. Northern Virginia had a reputation about being racist, not welcoming, whatever you want to call it. When I started to work for the federal government in 1974, I told young lawyers they ought to live in Alexandria. And they said, "That's in Virginia." They didn't want to live in Virginia. They would live in Washington or in Maryland but not in Virginia. I think that held back some of the progress we could make just because it exacerbated the difference between blacks and whites in terms of class structure.

Talk to me about individuals who were influential in preventing this from happening.

I had close personal contact with one. I can't remember his name. I came back here in 1974 and hadn't been here a month when the head of the Old Town Civic Association called me and said the Park and Recreation Commission has for a year had an opening for somebody from Old Town. He was looking for a patsy. The chairman told me about protesting when they paired T.C. Williams. He had been out there on the front line screaming at the buses and the black children when they got off the buses.

His kids had been at Hammond, which was mostly white, while George Washington was mostly black. He was apparently a leader of the opposition forces. I think later he realized what he had done was wrong. That it was bad for him personally and not good for the people who followed him. He had been on the Park and Recreation Commission for a long time.

Did you know Harvey Harrison?

Harvey Harrison, I knew him. He was on the school board a year or so after I got on. He was right wing. My first connection with him was when the board wanted to lessen the distance that kids had to walk to school. Harvey said he used to have a Boy Scout Troop and they had to walk two miles every Saturday and there's nothing wrong with these kids walking half a mile! That kind of attitude was pervasive, on every issue. Other board members laughed at him. I sat next to him and sat on the end because I was new. I had nobody else to talk to.

Allison May was our real estate agent when we rented our house in 1965. She was a very nice lady, of New England origin, a kind woman, and smart. Fred Day had been chair before I came. He was always on the positive side. He was a reasonable person with a reasoned view of the world. You couldn't get angry at him, because he wouldn't be angry with you.

On the positive side, who was influential in helping desegregation to succeed? Redistricting is always so unsettling.

I think there were parents on the other side who thought this was a good thing. There clearly were a lot of black people who saw it as a good thing, a culmination of the Brown vs. Board of Education decision. And the overturning of Plessy vs. Ferguson in 1893, that this was good. I think it is unfortunate that members of the black community thought perhaps we shouldn't have had integration, that we should go back to segregation. I think that sends the wrong message to our children. Parents who opposed pairing to get racial balance sent the wrong message. Things were not as bad as portrayed in that movie, *Remember the Titans,* but nevertheless it was not good. Those parents could have served their children better had they listened to reason and come at it with we can't maintain the status quo, we have to live with all people.

Final question. What do you think about the future?
Somebody asked my daughter the other day, "Where do you get all these facts in your head?" and she said, "You have to shove some facts out to make room for new." I will say this. She graduated from T.C. Williams in 1983 and went to Bryn Mawr College. Every time we would go to Bryn Mawr, one of the young women would tell us that of all the members of her class, she had the best preparation for college. These were young women who had attended prep schools throughout the East Coast, from foreign countries, and from out west, and they said nobody was better prepared to go to college than our daughter. I attribute that to our fine teachers and staff. So back to your question about staff. The teachers buckled down and said we've got a job to do and we're going to make it work. They were very instrumental in getting this done.

The future? I think I've seen some new things going on in the school system. One, the Lyles-Crouch school, for example, which for years had a terrible reputation, and there was talk of closing it because it had so few students. But there was an undercurrent, never from the black community, that you can never close Lyles-Crouch because it was a black school. It would be like closing Parker Gray.

Lyles-Crouch has turned itself into a traditional academy. It's wonderful to go by there and see those kids. Had I been on the School Board then, I'd probably have opposed it. But it brought back people, the kids all play together. There's no lottery to get into it. It's all local kids. I was a little dismayed about the failure to start what I proposed during my last couple of years on the school board—an arts specialty school where children learn by doing instead of listening and reading and watching. They don't really do that at Jefferson-Houston. That school has suffered for some reason. Specialty schools will go on for a while and enhance the school system for a few more years. We started with Cora Kelly—and it seemed to work because all the parents said "This is a special school."

The problem is every one will be a specialty school and eventually they're all going to come up to the top of the pyramid and it's not going to be the same at T.C. Williams. The kids who were wearing uniforms at Lyles-Crouch won't want to wear uniforms when they get to T.C. But the kids who go to Jefferson-Houston might want to. I want to see that the population will be interested in specialty schools. That will be the wave of the future for the short term.

There are other good teachers there who are going to retire. I hope we have good young teachers coming on. For a while it was not helpful to the teaching profession. When I was a kid, there were only two professions for women—teaching and library. Then the world opened up for them. It was gradual and I think that partly it was technology. Women for a long time were and probably are still the best computer programmers. So it's a whole new field, where women could be the equal of men. What it did was take women away from the teaching profession. Through elementary school I had one male teacher, in the sixth grade, the rest were all women. The principals were females until I got to high school. There were male teachers who taught shop and there were male science teachers. But men didn't teach history or English. In the future, as things settle down, the teaching profession will get better. I hope it will.

I think one of the changes that are taking place is that some of the union leaders have caught on. They realize that protecting everybody regardless is not the right way to go. They are working closer with management.

I hope so. That was not necessarily true when I was on the school board. Privately, the head of the union would sit down at the table and agree that this person is not doing a good job, but it's your job, not mine.

I had some rough experiences in the Philippines. But I was more frightened about facing my first class as a teacher than I was in the service.

Sure, you're thrown in there and you're in charge. The classroom has twenty-five diverse personalities that you know very little about except maybe their names. And it's a challenge for the kids. They ask themselves, "How can I beat the teacher?"

In the era when Page and I went to school, our twelfth-grade guidance counselor was also our chemistry teacher. Fifteen or twenty years ago I read in the paper that she had a business of helping kids get into college. How could she still be alive, we asked? She was probably only twenty-two years old, and we were sixteen or seventeen. We thought they were all at least forty. Teachers were truly gods and goddesses. Students as they get older know who the good teachers are.

Something like how dogs sense people. They recognize. You've got to know your stuff to teach.

They have an aura about them. They have control. They make it fun and interesting. If the teaching profession goes as I think it will, we will get better and better teachers. I see it with some of our brightest T.C. Williams High School graduates are coming back here to teach.

The rewards are there, they're not financial rewards but a wonderful feeling about helping students, keeping in touch. They stay in contact.

Bill Euille

Interviewed on August 15, 2006

Bill Euille is a lifelong resident of Alexandria who graduated from T.C. Williams in 1968 and is now serving his second term as mayor. He formerly served on the Alexandria School Board.

I'd like you to tell me where you grew up and how you arrived where you are today.

I was born in 1950 and grew up in Alexandria. We lived in public housing, in the area commonly known as the Berg. When I finished college in 1972 and returned here to Alexandria, I continued to live with my mom and my brother in public housing another couple of years and finally I had an opportunity to become a home owner. I purchased our first home in the Del Ray section of Alexandria in 1974 where I currently reside.

Recalling the Brown decision of 1954, I realize that you were not that old yet, but later in the 1950s you began to associate and understand what the reaction was in the city of Alexandria. Do you remember the reaction of any of your teachers in those early days?

I had grown up here and attended grades 1 to 7 at the all-black Lyles-Crouch Elementary School. Alexandria had only two elementary schools available to blacks at that time. Charles Houston was for kids on the north side of the city. Kids that lived down in the Berg and in the southern end of city (Old Town) went to Lyles-Crouch. We walked every day (there was no bus transportation down to the Berg to pick us up, so we walked through all the elements—rain, sleet, and snow) to get to school. In our neighborhood, we would walk past the "all-white" Ficklin Elementary School, just a few blocks away, to get to Lyles-Crouch. En route to Lyles-Crouch, some kids who lived on the south side walked by the all-white Prince Street and Lee Elementary to get to school. That was during normal school hours.

The irony was that when school let out and we were all back in our respective neighborhoods, we played together on playgrounds and in other parts of the city, in public parks. Black and white kids were all playing together and having fun together. It never occurred to us that there was anything wrong with the fact that we all went to separate schools. You were born and raised and taught—this was the norm.

Back then in elementary school there were signs that I had the potential to become a leader to the extent that I was a class officer, student patrol officer, and an academic achiever. I had the responsibility of being the school photographer at Lyles-Crouch.

One day my principal, Mrs. Hilton, received a phone call request from the principal at Lee Elementary asking if we had a camera. Lee was having a science fair and they needed to take some pictures. The principal at Lyles-Crouch said. "Yes, we can lend it to you. The Lee principal said, "We'll send somebody over to pick it up," and Mrs. Hilton said, "We'll do even better than that. I'll have our school photographer walk over and bring it to your school and while he's there he'll be able to take the pictures for you."

The principal summoned for me to come to her office. "Bill, the principal at Lee needs a photographer," she told me, "and I said I would send you over." That was fine with me. I was in the seventh grade and mature enough to walk by myself to Lee, a few blocks away. So as I was walking there, my initial reaction was "Boy, this is going to be interesting. I'm leaving my all-black school to go to this all-white school, which I've never been inside of before. I will see kids I play with every day on the playground." I wondered what would be my reaction, and their reaction, to this exposure.

I reported to the office and the principal greeted me and took me to one or two classrooms to take pictures. I'll be honest with you. Other than the fact that I knew I was in a different environment, it really had no effect, positively or negatively, on me because as I looked around, I saw kids that I knew. They respected and appreciated me being in their school. No one said, "What are you doing here? This isn't your school!"

It was so unfortunate that we were segregated at that time by schools, but fortunate that in the community we found an opportunity to play together and socialize.

When you went to Connecticut to college, did you encounter any discrimination?

I attended a small coed private college, Quinnipiac, in the town of Hamden, Connecticut, which is north of New Haven and south of Hartford. It was situated on a very beautiful campus at the foot of a state park, Sleeping Giant Mountain.

I went there because Quinnipiac offered me a full academic scholarship. None of the other schools I applied to offered me any financial aid, and I wouldn't have been able to go at all because my family certainly couldn't afford it. So this was an opportunity and I took advantage of it. My parents could not accompany me to Connecticut the first day I reported to school for three reasons: (1) We didn't have the financial means to drive up by car, (2) they couldn't afford to go up on the train with me, and (3) they had to stay here and work. So I went on the train by myself with my big footlocker and other luggage.

I arrived at the Amtrak station in New Haven, got a taxi, and told the driver I needed to go to Quinnipiac College. He knew exactly where to go. I had not previously visited the school campus subsequent to my acceptance and much to my surprise, it wasn't what I thought it would be. I thought maybe I had made a mistake. I expected to see large buildings, but I saw only a few small buildings. The taxi driver was told this was as far as he could go. So I unloaded my things, paid the driver, and proceeded to get my luggage into the dorm. When I arrived at the front entrance at the dorm I was assigned to, they greeted me, asked me my name, and said, "Oh, you're on third floor. Here is your room key." I looked around the halls and put my luggage in my room. Of course you didn't bother to unpack right away. You were excited, being there on the first day with all the other students arriving with their families.

We were told to go outside and socialize and enjoy the cookout. Then there was going to be an orientation meeting and we would get our marching orders. While outside attempting to meet people, within fifteen or twenty minutes I heard my name being called by two administrators. One was the dean of students, Bob Evans, who became my very personal and close friend and mentor. The other administrator was Don Blumenthal, director of housing. When they found me they asked that I accompany them to my room. I asked what I had done wrong. I'd been there only fifteen minutes and I'm in trouble, I thought. "No, you're not in trouble," they said.

In the room was a family—a white family—mother, father, and son. They introduced me to the family so I greeted them. Then the administrators asked the family to leave the room and they shut the door. Then the dean and the housing director asked about my background, about my family and what kind of work my father did, and so forth. I answered their questions and I asked, "What is this all about?"

They told me that the family of the young man who was to be my roommate had problems with him rooming with an African-American. Of 1100 students there, I learned there were fewer than thirty minorities on the whole campus.

I stated that I personally didn't have a problem rooming with a white student, after all, I attended a fully integrated public high school, T.C. Williams High School. I said I would stay in this room or they could assign me to another room. Without even hesitating, they said no, they were not going to do that. Then I left the room and the family came back in. In a few moments, the family left the room, taking their son's luggage. I asked the dean and the director of housing what was happening and they said "You're staying here. We'll get you a new roommate. The family has chosen to withdraw their son from the school." I said I didn't mean to cause a problem, and they said "No, we don't want people here with a racial attitude."

That experience really prepared me to become the person I am today. I decided I wanted to run for freshman class president, though nobody knew me at all. Lo and behold, not only did I become the president of the freshman class, but also president of the sophomore class, and president of student government as a junior. I was Mr. Who's Who on campus and I graduated with a degree in accounting and returned to Alexandria.

When did you lose your father?

My father died in 1985. While I was in elementary school, my father and mother separated. He was an alcoholic, not a good family man. I was probably ten or eleven when they separated. He still lived in the city and I saw him often. My mother spent the rest of her young adult life raising three kids by herself, something very challenging.

Let's go now to the famous 2-2-2 plan in Alexandria. What was the reaction from the school community and from school personnel?

I graduated from T.C. Williams in 1968, when the entire school enrollment was probably 20,000+. The schools had been fully integrated for three years, and things were working well. While I was away at college I received the local newspaper (*The*

Alexandria Gazette), and started to hear about white flight and a declining public school enrollment. By the time I had graduated, in 1972, the school board had decided to reorganize the schools, going to a 6-2-2-2 plan. So students went to an elementary school for six years, then two years to a seventh- and eighth-grade school, then to another one for grades nine and ten, and then to T.C. Williams for eleventh and twelfth grades.

I assumed that the professional staff, the school board, and the community knew best. When I came back to Alexandria in 1972 and began working and became active, I realized the schools were having problems. Things were not working, the school system was not successful. We needed to shore up the public schools and be more responsive, while maintaining an integrated school system. The neighborhoods were beginning to move into integration, so I decided to get involved. I felt that I had received an excellent education from a school system that helped me prepare for success in college and I thought maybe I could offer some insights. Instead of being a critic, I worked to make change. I got involved.

So at the very tender age of twenty-four, I applied for a seat on the school board and the City Council appointed me. I served for ten long years, trying to stop the bleeding; healing, and moving forward. I liked to think that we accomplished just that. And here it is, more than thirty years later, and we have indeed made progress. The school board has retooled the system twice since I left the school board—for the good. Presently, all of the sixteen schools are now fully integrated.

You were on the school board that hired me. They were quite a group.
Unlike today, school boards then were not politicized, they were appointed by City Council. The members were very diverse, representing various opinions of the community. We listened to the community. We had our challenges, not only dealing with

the declining enrollment but also budgeting issues and others. Folks for the most part still wanted their own community schools again, so redistricting went out the window and we had to find another solution. It was so difficult during my ten-year tenure on the board to balance all the wants and needs and challenges. We were blessed because we had you, Bob. You came from Stamford, Connecticut, to take the helm of being superintendent. You brought a lot of insight and were very positive. You were cause oriented, and that helped the board and the community to move in the right direction.

You did things to make sure that changes were implemented in the right way. Dr. John C. Abohm was the longest tenured superintendent in the city, and you, Bob Peebles, were the third longest the city has ever had. You came in and you got the job done and you left when your task was accomplished. We're grateful to you for that.

Who would you identify as key in helping the community and make this huge change, both in the community and in the schools?
We had lots of good community activists from the African-American community, not only names like Ferdinand Day, Melvin Miller, and Nelson Green. We had ministers from the black churches, and other non-African-Americans like Mel Bergheim on City Council, Mayor Chuck Beatley, and ministers of all-white churches. It was done in a broad-based community spirit way. We all came together. We have a wonderful opportunity here in Alexandria in that it has always been a caring community, a city of opportunity. Folks really came together to say we're going to make it work, we're going to do what's right.

I think that lots of the success we enjoy today, not only in the schools but in the city as a whole, we had some key stakeholders, many of them were not even natives. Some came here for employment or were in the military, but they saw Alexandria as one place in this country where people could come together and share their differences and heal. Alexandria was that place. I've been grateful these many years later for what the past has led us to.

I constantly advocate today that despite our successes, we still have many challenges, but the way we meet out challenges is by working together in unity as a family. We are fortunate that we have broad-based support, not only from the business community but also from faith-based groups and the non-profits, and our diversity continues to grow. We are a growing city of 140,000 people, with more than 50 percent of the population being non-Caucasian.

Who do you remember on the other side of coin as obstructions who tried for it to fail?

Before you came here as superintendent a Colonel Wilford Smith, a resident of Old Town, served on the school board with me. He was one of a few who was very negative. His reason for serving on the board was to express a certain opinion, but at the same time he didn't work to make things better. His major role was to belittle and beat up the school system, to tear down what we were working to rebuild. So when his term ended, members of City Council and other members of the community realized he was not what we needed on the board. I actually got to know him more and we had our "come-to-Jesus" discussions. But all in all, he was a nice person.

What about the school personnel—do you recall anybody who did what they could to obstruct the desegregation implementation?

Not any administrators, but probably a few teachers. I do recall that no matter what progress we made, there were always a few teachers who felt that "those people" will never make it in our society, and they don't want to learn. They were few and far between, but we had a lot of professional teachers who were very supportive of these efforts. They were in education as a career and they realized that times were changing and they were taught not to teach to color but to teach to human beings.

Do some predictions. Where do you see us headed on the race issue?

We're fortunate in Alexandria in that we are seeing growth in our population. We also see some stability in the African-American population, which was declining at one point and was impacted by the lack of affordable housing. We're seeing a shift in middle class families, and at the same time we see a growth in the Hispanic population, a rapid growth at that, and other ethnicities and immigrants are moving in. While there is still much more to do, we're making progress at it.

I recall reading a few weeks ago that the overall minority population in the United States now is almost 50 percent. The minorities have actually become the majority, because of the diversity, our shifting population, and rapid expansion. It is not going anyplace, it's here to stay. So people need a paradigm or attitude shift to accept the current or future status in terms of where we're going to go. The whole global economy is out there—it's not changing. My travels outside the U.S. during these past five or six years have convinced me that no matter where you go in the world, the only difference between folks is culture and language.

I was in Istanbul, Turkey, a few weeks ago. I didn't know what to expect. I went over with some Turkish friends of mine who have lived in the United States for thirty years. Upon my arrival I sensed no animosity. Tourism is a big trade industry, and people were excited to see me. When I walked through their malls, they said, "You're an American. Are you a body builder?" I said no, but they said, "You've got to be a body builder. Look at you!"

They wanted to dialog with me. The common bond that we had was that whether they were Russian or Iraqi they knew

I was from a nation that is trying to spread our wings and try to govern and advocate for democracy. They saw me as a positive symbol that all Americans are not bad people. They have their own perceptions of us. When you sit and talk with them they say "We love Americans, it's your political leaders that cause us pain and anger."

I think the future of race relations, not only in this country but in the world, is moving in the right direction, but we must fully understand the need for all of us to live on this great earth together, to survive, to live together. We need to view each and every one of us as a family. Yes, families have their differences, but like most families, you keep them internal. You work them out, you don't air your problems in public. When we learn to understand, appreciate, and love each other, then we will survive.

Sports and music are two great integrators. If you blow well, it doesn't make any difference, you're part of that group.

In Turkey you hear Turkish and ethnic music. I thought I was back here in the United States when I heard music on an FM station there that could have been the same music you would hear here in Washington or in New York or Los Angeles. They dress like we do, the kids wear baggy jeans, their baseball caps are turned the wrong way. I was there while the World Cup and the Miss America pageant were going on. Then you had the crisis between Israel and Lebanon brewing. At the pageant, folks were saying the contestants are going to have to stand on the stage together tomorrow night. The fact remains that they did stand next to each other, just like sports or music. It's something we can all understand. We can socialize and play together. Wouldn't it be nice if politics were a sport? A lot of our world issues would go right out the door if we did it in a fun way instead of aggression. That doesn't gain you anything but conflict.

Christine Howard

Interviewed on June 22, 2006

Christine Howard grew up in Alexandria and became an elementary teacher and principal in city schools. She has created educational and training programs for her church. She has traveled around the globe but is now retired.

I would like you to tell me where you grew up, how you arrived in Alexandria, and where you are now.
   I was born in Alexandria. I have lived here all of my life. I've always been very proud to be able to teach at home, and now that I'm retired it is my time to do things I want to do in life. I've been able to do that. A very successful career has allowed me to make this truly my time. I've been very fortunate to do something I loved, working here in Alexandria.

After the famous decision of 1954 declaring segregated schools unconstitutional in Alexandria, what was the reaction of the community and school people at that time in 1954, in the 50s?
   Alexandria seemed to have taken integration calmly. We had a few problems, but not a lot of anger, knowing that we deserved the right to attend any school in Alexandria. That was the attitude of the majority of the black community. School people were given their assignments. I was transferred from Charles Houston School to the Prince Street School. My mother believed strongly that you should treat people like you wanted to be treated. So I called each parent and said, "My name is Christine Howard and I will be your child's teacher.

And I am black." Children enrolled in Prince Street School came from John Roberts' public housing. One parent said to me, "As long as you are a good teacher, I don't care what color you are."

Bill Bryant was the principal. He was good with the children and I was helpful to him. It was one of the best years of my teaching career. The Prince Street School closed at the end of the school year and I went to Minnie Howard.

When I was getting certified to teach, my mother passed away and I was unable to complete my courses at Virginia State. The superintendent, T.C. Williams, told me not to worry. I was shocked because he fought desegregation so bitterly. That was a side of him I didn't know. "You will work," he said. "I won't give you a contract but I'll give you the salary." And that's what I did that year.

From Minnie Howard I went to Theodore Ficklin School and worked with Lucy Kirby, who was the principal there. This was in 1968. I decided I needed a master's and I applied to the University of Virginia. I applied to Alexandria City Public Schools for a sabbatical and it was granted. I went to the University of Virginia, where I lived on campus. I was the first black to live on campus and I was the only black in my classes in 1969. I was there a year and got my degree. It was a beautiful experience and a beautiful campus.

The only negative experience I had there was when I went to register. I went to the person in charge and he said, "You have to get in line here." I only wanted to ask a question.

After that day I enjoyed every minute. It was a good experience. Graduation was held on the lawn. Each graduate stood for one second at the top of the steps of the Rotunda, looking up at a beautiful blue sky. I said to myself, "Here I am standing, achieving a goal that I wanted." I'll always have fond memories of the University.

Chris, go back to the 1950s again, and tell me the reaction of school personnel, administrators, teachers, everybody.

I personally felt that each morning when the children stepped into the classroom I thought "I care about you as a person." Then along came integration, and we had many workshops to prepare teachers and administrators for this day. But you can't do that. It doesn't work. It has to come from within. You can have all the workshops in the world but you cannot prepare a person to teach a kid that over the years has been told "You are not going to be successful."

It never really worked, trying to prepare administrators and teachers. You can't do that, it has to be within that person. Some teachers had this special gift for dealing with all the children, but many were not prepared. Because of that, many children suffered.

Who in the community was very influential in efforts to kill the desegregation effort?

I don't remember the real ugliness of it.

Any school board members? The School Board that hired me was Alison May, Shirley Tyler, Lou Cook, and Judy Feaver—good people. Who would you say on the positive side was very helpful, positive, influential in making it work?

Connie Ring. Ferdinand Day. I tried desperately to stay away from politics.

There tends to be more involvement in politics at the secondary level, that's generally true. Remember the Titans. That's quite a story. It made a millionaire out of Boone and maybe Bill Yoast. That was quite a movie, and it's still being shown. That was quite a step that Albohm made with that plan, I think, making T.C. the city's single high school. Quite dramatic. What was the reaction in Alexandria to that plan?

Unfortunately, teachers don't want to leave their comfort zone, but they had to. Hammond was not a happy school, oh no. Neither Hammond nor G.W. had any black students until Parker Gray was closed in 1965. Parker Gray was a very good high school, a segregated school. But there were too many positive advantages to Dr. Albohm's plan.

Albohm made some statements that turned the black community off to him, but the longer he stayed the more they came to understand him. He did not go over well in the black community.

One influential group was the Departmental Progressive Club. It was also political, and had a lot of influence. I forgot to mention Helen Day. She taught at Charles Houston.

I've been told that you and Ardelia Hunter had to go to D.C. schools at one point when Alexandria was fully segregated.

My older sisters had to go into D.C. Beyond eighth grade. They attended Dunbar, Armstrong, and a trade school in D.C. Dunbar has quite an alumni group. I did not have to go into D.C., and Ardelia did not. We finished at Parker Gray.

My last question: This is your opportunity to give me your ideas as to what you think will happen in the future to our schools.

I watch the schools today and I firmly believe that schools must have an opportunity for success. I see parental involvement in some schools but not enough involvement in schools needing it the most. The population of our schools has become more diverse. We are preparing students to be world leaders. Schools must prepare today's students to be contributing, responsible citizens in a highly competitive and technological society.

Excellence in education requires parents, students, teachers, and administrators to assume their responsibilities in the learning process. High quality education must be our goal if we expect one of the nation's greatest resources, our youth, to meet tomorrow's challenges confidently and effectively. We are not there yet!

Mark Howard

Interviewed on May 19, 2006

Mark Howard served as an administrator at Alexandria's three secondary schools for 26 years. Since retiring in 1993, he has become an avid golfer.

Mark, tell me where you grew up and how you got to where you are now.

I'm from New England. I was born in Marblehead, Massachusetts, a small coastal town on the North Shore, 18 miles north of Boston. I lived there until I was ten years old. Our house sat on a hill, and my bedroom, which I shared with my brother, overlooked the harbor. I remember what a beautiful sight the harbor was in the summer and how cold it looked in the winter.

Like so many people, the occurrence of a catastrophic event changes their lives. My life in Marblehead was changed with that infamous date of December 7, 1941. My father was a yachtsman and a yacht broker—he sold boats. He grew up around boats and knew a great deal about boats. His experience and knowledge of boats drew the attention of the Maritime Commission in Washington, D.C. In the early summer of 1942, the family left Marblehead and moved to Washington. We settled in a community called Wesley Heights, near American University, a long way from my little town of Marblehead.

Initially, it was a very sad time for me. I quickly made new friends, discovered new activities, and attended new schools. I lived in this neighborhood for sixteen years, graduating from

Woodrow Wilson High School in 1951. I was active in athletics—I was on the wrestling team and was the frontline pitcher on the baseball team my senior year. I got to pitch at the old Griffith Stadium my senior year in a semifinal playoff game. What a thrill it was for me to stand on the pitcher's mound of a big league ballpark and just look around the stadium! It was an awesome experience. I had beaten this team earlier in the season but lost this time. But the joy of this experience for the kid from Marblehead lingers on.

After graduating from high school I planned to attend the University of Virginia, but my mother was not happy with this decision. She thought I would be more successful in a smaller school—that is, small class sizes and closer contact with the professors. My church minister arranged an interview for me at Dickinson College in Carlisle, Pennsylvania. A week after that interview with the dean of admissions I received a letter of acceptance. I loved my experience at Dickinson. I was a history major with a minor in political science.

Tragedy struck me in my senior year. My mother died. She was a strong influence in my life and was my guidance counselor. I had no idea what I wanted to do after I graduated. My mother had suggested several times that I should be a teacher. Even my aunt echoed this same suggestion. And surprisingly to me, one of my college professors had said the same thing. In response to him, I said I did not want to teach in a public school. His reply to me was, "I don't mean in a public school but in a prep school." Now that certainly put a new twist on the matter.

In September of 1955 I entered Georgetown University Law School. I had a good year. Most memorable for me was when I was called on in class by the professor more than halfway through the course to recite a case. With more than 125 students in the class, and me shaking to beat the band, I stood up and gave my recitation, then sat down. The professor seemed to pause a long time as he looked around the class. Finally he said, "That was the finest recitation I've heard this year!" That was such a morale and confidence booster. But it was not enough for me to continue in law school and I was not sure I wanted to be a lawyer. Besides, nobody had told me I should be a lawyer.

I went into the Army for two years following my one year in law school. It was an interesting two years. I was acting platoon sergeant in basic training and a typing instructor for eight weeks in a clerk/administrative class. Yes, I was a teacher for the first time. I loved it. Finally I was assigned to Fort Myer, Virginia, for the remainder of my tour of duty. After eighteen months of duty in Washington, D.C., I was discharged. While doing duty in Washington, I was married.

After a year of fumbling around in the banking and insurance business, I still had not found my vocational niche. I finally said to myself, "Mark, what have you enjoyed the most in your work experience?" You guessed it. My mother, my aunt, and my college professor were right—teaching. Commanding forty men in basic training as an acting sergeant and teaching a typing class in an army training class brought out in me a command presence before a group of learners that I enjoyed. To see these "students" become learners and advance in their performance due to my leadership was very satisfying to me. So I mentioned to my wife that I think I would like to teach. She talked with a friend where she worked about my interest in a teaching career. The friend was the daughter of Alexandria's school superintendent, T.C. Williams. Within a few days I was sitting in Ray Sanger's office being interviewed.

I remember Joe McGowan walking by and Mr. Sanger saying, "Joe, come in here. I've got another New Englander here." Well, the interview went well. Mr. Sanger said Hammond High School needed a social studies teacher and he would be contacting me shortly. I also had an interview at St. Stephen's the next day. (There's that prep school again.) That interview went well, also. Their offering salary was $800 lower than Alexandria's.

When I said to the interviewer at St. Stephens that his salary was $800 lower than the salary I was being offered by Alexandria, he said, "Well, in this case, the milk is lighter at the bottom of the bottle and you have to wait until the cream comes to the top."

Well, I could accept his metaphor but not his salary. Fortunately, Ray Sanger called me the next day to say that I was hired to be a U.S. history and U.S. government teacher at Francis C. Hammond High School. My teaching career had begun, albeit in a public school.

On November 1, 1961, I began a six-year teaching career at Hammond and what a joyful and rewarding experience that was for me! The school had many excellent teachers, many fine students, and a friendly and very comfortable atmosphere. I knew I had finally found my vocational niche.

Having earned my master's degree from The George Washington University in 1965, I was now ready to move into school administration if the opportunity arose, and it did in 1967. The Alexandria School Board, under the leadership of its new school superintendent, Dr. John C. Albohm, had completed its first major desegregation plan in 1966. But problems of desegregation persisted throughout most of the city but most egregiously in the eastern section of the city due to the 1966 plan's reliance on neighborhood school assignments. A large proportion of the black population lived in this section of the city, so their children were assigned to attend the white schools located in this section.

I think Dr. Albohm was hoping that a new team of administrators would assuage a steaming unrest in local white neighborhoods in the George Washington High School zone, and that by incorporating many new human relations programs for all city administrators and teachers, improved human relations skills would benefit all. HEW and the Office of Civil Rights saw little hope that this plan would satisfy the Supreme Court's

Brown ruling and the District of Columbia's District Court's Bolling ruling. But gratefully, HEW was dilatory in its enforcement. The western end of the city, where the more affluent neighborhoods were, suffered little under the 1966 plan.

So in 1967 I went to George Washington as an assistant principal, along with another new assistant principal and a new principal. While at G.W., I also became director of the adult evening program that was housed there.

We had many good teachers at G.W., both black and white, and many good students, both black and white. But the major role of the assistant principal was to handle the discipline of the persistently recalcitrant students who constantly disrupted classroom decorum. I'd go home at night saying to myself that I couldn't continue to be someone else's whipping boy. I felt my job was not fulfilling and not rewarding. Upon my request in 1970, I was transferred to T.C. Williams High School as an assistant principal. I probably was hoping that a change in schools would change my outlook.

The discipline problems were not as pervasive at T.C. as they were at G.W. Should I say because there were fewer black students there? Was there better leadership there? I don't know; I do remember one instance that has "stuck in my craw" till this day.

One morning I was in my office with a student when the principal came by and asked me to go out on the front porch and direct the five or six black students standing out there to get on to class. He said he would go around the back way and meet them should they deviate from a direct path to their class. I went out to the students and directed them into the building and to move on to class. Begrudgingly, they complied. Then the principal emerged from around the back hall. I told him they had gone to class.

Now why didn't he, as principal, handle this matter? Anyway, he left T.C. the following year. Incidentally, I started my doctoral program while at T.C. Unknown to me at this time, the reorganization of all the secondary schools was in the planning stages in the central office.

After one year at T.C., I was sent back to G.W. as assistant principal and Steve Osisek was made principal. With the adoption of the 2-2-2 reorganization plan for the secondary schools, G.W. was now a ninth and tenth grade school. After the first year, Mr. Osisek named me the associate principal. I remained in that position at G.W. until June 1989. In the last three months of the 1973–74 school year, I was acting principal as Mr. Osisek went on medical leave. He retired in June 1987 and Bob Yeager was appointed principal. I remained the associate principal.

Two years later all administrators except one were transferred to other schools. Bob Yeager went back to T.C. as the associate principal and I was transferred to Hammond as an assistant principal. Tony Hanley brought in his own administrative staff. Near the close of the 1989–90 school year, Mr. Hanley contacted me at Hammond and asked me if I could come back to G.W. and help him. I said I would only if I came back as an associate principal. He said he would check with the superintendent. He called me back a day or two later and said the superintendent said all right. That gave G.W. two associate principals.

I returned to G.W. in late August 1990. In the first faculty meeting Mr. Hanley announced my presence and said that I was returning to G.W. Many teachers applauded and cheered. Boy!!! That unexpected reception made me feel awfully good. During one of the in-service days at G.W., the superintendent, who was in the school, saw me and came over to shake my hand and welcome me back to G.W. I was beginning my 22nd year at G.W.

Well, I don't know why but at the end of the school year, the superintendent transferred all the administrators out of G.W. and again, I was sent to Hammond for the 1991–92 school year to manage the computer lab. I hung in there for one year and then retired in 1993.

Recall your impressions of what Alexandria was like when the court order came and you had to do something.

I'm not sure which court order the question refers to, but my research says the School Board and Superintendent Williams took the position that they were to follow the laws of Virginia and maintain a segregated school system. The League of Women Voters took the position of supporting the immediate implementation of the 1955 ruling. There were some citizens who supported a move to get along with some desegregation plan.

Superintendent Williams was a hard-line states-rightist and followed the course of Virginia law. Dr. Albohm, not a Virginian, knew the School Board had to begin accepting the authority of federal law, but he and the school board didn't really know what to do. Pressure was on him and the school board from the NAACP and from the vocal groups of residents in the eastern section of the city to begin eliminating "with all deliberate speed" the segregated school system and the unfairness of assigning students to schools by neighborhoods.

Dr. Albohm was looking for guidance from HEW to help steer him and the school board into an acceptable desegregation plan. This could have been a very smart delaying tactic by Dr. Albohm, allowing him and the school board to gain some breathing room. With the K6-2-2-2 and the elementary school desegregation plans, Dr. Albohm and the school board worked aggressively to satisfy the guidelines of HEW and save the city more than two million dollars. Neither plan could have been implemented without the results of the Swann decision and its dictum, which gave approval of busing as a way to transport students across neighborhood lines.

What was Alexandria like as a community, and the school community itself? How did teachers respond? You came here as a Yankee.

I came into the school system in 1961. At that time I was living in Washington, D.C. I moved to Alexandria in the summer of 1962 and lived in Parkfairfax. In 1964 I moved to Fairfax County, Springfield. Teachers at Hammond talked very little about desegregation. Though Hammond had two black students enter the school in 1959, all went quite smoothly.

The initial organization of Alexandria's schools along HEW guidelines for racial parity was in 1965. The neighborhood school concept was the basis for assigning all students to their school. Since the vast majority of blacks lived in the eastern sector of the city and that is where the black high school was located, the white schools, and particularly G.W., absorbed the vast majority of black students in the city.

Hostility pervaded among many blacks as well as among many whites in the G.W. community. Leaders in the Del Ray and Rosemont communities bitterly complained that the teachers' standards were being lowered and poor student discipline among the blacks was a disrupting influence at G.W.

Many teachers were extremely frustrated. My experience at G.W. from 1967 to 1970 evidenced to me that it was only a small minority of blacks who continually caused problems. There was hostility among some of the black students and black parents. Both felt they were not getting fair treatment and that the white teachers discriminated against them.

At a night football game at G.W. against Hammond, many parents were there. After the game, which was won by Hammond, a few white Hammond parents complained about being jostled and harassed as they came out of the bleachers and walked through the parking lot. This caused consternation among these parents and, I feel, reverberations in the Hammond community, the western sector of the city, that they wanted no part of desegregation. Much of this anti-integration attitude was displayed by a hostile group of parents the night the school board voted at T.C. Williams to adopt the reorganization plan for secondary schools.

What about individuals in the city? Non-teachers, non-school people. Do you remember who played a significant role in that?
No one particular person. I wasn't privy to a lot of the communication between Steve Osisek and the parents. The president of the Del Ray community and the Rosemont community met with him many times. I do not recall seeing a black community leader meeting with him.

How about the Old Town liberals who wanted it to succeed? The Bigelows and the Elliotts and others?
I am not aware of any Old Town liberals who wanted desegregation to succeed, but citywide desegregation could not have succeeded without strong liberal support throughout the city as the K6-2-2-2 was a citywide plan.

Do you recall any individuals who actively tried to prevent this from happening? School or community people?
Connie Ring was a conservative, and I have a lot of respect for him. He was unwilling to go all at once toward integration. He frequently spoke that desegregation would be less dramatic if it were done grade by grade. I'm not sure that approach would have satisfied the "with all deliberate speed" mandate.
A resident of the western section of Alexandria, a William J. Sando, who did not take issue with the principle of the Brown decision but he and others were opposed to the concept of racial balance as implied in the Swann decision and the use of busing as a "vehicle" to accomplish it. Mr. Sando was the vice-president of a group of more than 1,000 members. He, however, did not think the leadership of the group was anti-integration. Most of its members lived in the western section of the city. He went to court to block the 2-2-2 plan. The court said the plan was

constitutionally permissible. Mr. Sando threatened to move out of Alexandria.

What do you think it's going to be like in the future? In 2006, look at the student makeup, the ethnic, racial, and cultural forces interacting daily.

Students now and in the future will be living in a more global environment. Nations are becoming more dependent on one another for economic goods. Rapid transportation, internet communications, and television will allow peoples of the world to talk with one another and see different cultures and people from a range of ethnic, racial, and social backgrounds. Many of these people are in our country today and are met at the grocery store or place of business every day. And we are in theirs. The intermingling of the world's people will help for a better understanding of their differences and the identification of their commonalities. Fears and distrust generated by ignorance, hopefully, will evaporate and a brotherhood of nations will slowly emerge.

The future always belongs to those who have yet to live it. Education for everyone in common and equally shared environments is the best way to prepare all the youth for their adventure into a world of global neighborhoods.

Gilbert Mays

Interviewed August 9, 2006

Dr. Mays served in the Virginia State Department of Education before coming to Alexandria in 1970 as Assistant Principal at T.C. Williams High School. He was principal at the Minnie Howard Middle School before his retirement in 1985.

Gil, I'd like you to tell me where you grew up and how you ended up in Alexandria.

I grew up in southside Virginia, in Brunswick County. Lawrenceville was the little town we lived near. We lived on a tobacco farm, and I went to high school at St. Paul's Normal Industrial School, the only secondary school in the county for blacks. There was no public school at all for blacks after seventh grade, and no buses for public schools. Black families bought buses on which black students could ride to St. Paul's, for a fee.

I finished high school at St. Paul's and took two years of college there, finishing in 1939. In 1940 I went into the service and stayed till 1945. I was a driver in the Army quartermaster corps. I drove the post ambulances for two years.

I enjoyed the Army and I learned a lot. Camp Holabird (in Maryland) was originally established as an Army motor transport training center and depot. I was one of the black soldiers stationed there in the all-black company. Two other soldiers and I tested the prototype of the Army Jeep. Each of us drove over the testing area on eight-hour shifts until completion. Checker Cab engineers were in charge of the testing.

One day four or five newsreel companies came to Fort Holabird to do a story about this new vehicle. When they saw that we drivers were all black, one of them said, "We can't film black guys testing jeeps and show the film in white movie theaters," but the man from Pathe News said, "Wait a minute! These boys have been driving eight-hour shifts in freezing weather all winter long, and now you want to get white boys from the 23rd Regiment to come over so you can film them? Well, we won't do it."

So they all stayed an hour and talked and finally decided they would film us and the white soldiers. White soldiers were shown testing the jeep in white theaters and we were shown in the black theaters. That was segregation, too. The nation as a whole would never have known that black soldiers tested that vehicle. Ford built some of them, and other companies did, too.

Late in 1941, we were on maneuvers in North Carolina, near Pinehurst, with the First Army Regiment. On completing maneuvers in late November, our company drove non-stop to New York City. We had all the First Army records and money so we couldn't stop anywhere, except for gassing up. We got to New York on a Friday, and that Sunday we got the announcement that the Japanese had bombed Pearl Harbor. I spent eighteen months in England and Europe with the Third Army under General Patton until June 1945.

I got out of the Army in 1945 and then I came back to St. Paul's and finished college on the GI bill. I received my bachelor's degree in 1952 and then taught general science at James Solomon Russell High School in Brunswick County for five years. In 1957 I got a fellowship to go to the University of Virginia and I got a master's degree in science education. At the end of that academic year, I was appointed Assistant Supervisor of Science Education at the Virginia State Department of Education in 1958.

Did you and Albohm ever discuss race?
　　He was concerned about what was going on in the State Department of Education. He got desegregation done here and it worked. There was a big difference between him and the previous superintendent, T.C. Williams. He would not have hired me.

Dr. Albohm knew how to deal with the community.
　　They bumped him all right but he could handle it. I hear Connie Ring was rough on Albohm. All of his kids came through Minnie Howard when I was principal there and he was one of the best supporters. We sat down and talked. He was a conservative, and maybe he was against integration but I didn't see it. I don't think he was. He always complimented me. He would rather have had integration start in the elementary schools and phase it in gradually, but that was sort of like putting it off.

Tell me about the governor then.
　　The year I was at the University, in 1957, was the year of the school problem at Little Rock, Arkansas. We were looking at TV one night and the governor of Virginia was being interviewed. Someone asked him if there were any blacks at the University of Virginia. He said he didn't know but he hoped not. Actually, there was another black student there in addition to me—James Benton. We occupied the same dormitory room. We were the only two black graduate students and I think there was one undergraduate student in an undergraduate dormitory that same year.
　　When I was in graduate school, I was still living in Brunswick County with my wife and child, so I would drive home after Friday's classes and back to Charlottesville every Monday morning. We had no problems. I lived in the dormitory on campus during the week.

From there I went to the Virginia State Department of Education as an assistant supervisor of science education for black schools in Virginia. I was there till 1970, when I came to Alexandria as assistant principal at T.C. Williams High School. Dr. Albohm was the superintendent.

I was at T.C. until 1972, when I was appointed principal at the Minnie Howard Middle School. I stayed there until 1979, when I went back to T.C. as associate principal. I stayed there until 1985 when I retired. I was elected president of the Virginia Secondary School Principals Association in 1975.

That was during my watch. Gil, I'd like you to give me your impression of the reaction of the community and the city of Alexandria, the citizens, and also the school staff, to the court order to desegregate.

Well, I was in Brunswick County then, and nobody paid any attention to integration. I went to the University of Virginia in 1957. Things changed when I went to Richmond and was a science supervisor for the state. I worked primarily with black schools. A white supervisor worked with white schools. We did meet together at times, so integration moved rather slowly. When I was in the state department, it was all very separate. We had statewide meetings that were segregated. Before I left we began to meet together, about 1969. It took a long time.

When I came to Alexandria to work at T.C. Williams, Alexandria had three middle schools—Minnie Howard, John Adams, and Parker-Gray. Parker-Gray had been the city's black high school—and a very good one.

Do you remember any individuals in the community who did all they could to prevent desegregation from happening—or any school staff?

I didn't run into any of that, strange to say, from my own experience. People I worked with were all very cooperative. But I knew there was some opposition.

On the other side, who was active in trying to make it work in the community and in the schools?

White people were the ones who wanted to make it work, and the school board. I had no contact with the community except when the kids had problems. They seemed to be in favor of what we were trying to do at T.C. They were very cooperative. I had no problem whatsoever there. As far as I was concerned, things went very smoothly.

How about kids?

I didn't have to send many kids home. We'd sit down and talk. That's what they needed, someone to talk to. They were experiencing change and were not prepared to deal with it. So it was hard to figure out how to deal with it. That was my role at T.C. Williams, working with students.

You had a good staff at T.C.—John Porter, Roosevelt Peebles, Hollis Williams.

Yes, we were the class assistant principals.

And Tony Hanley was a good principal.

We all worked together. I had 11th grade students but I was not fixed there. I could work with 10th graders if they wanted to come to me.

Was there any kind of association of black educators in Alexandria?

Not really. Informally, there were social clubs in the community.

The Departmental Progressive Club was pretty influential.

I never did join it. I went to their functions and I knew their members.

My last question is to ask you to reflect on where you think all this is going. Where will we wind up in the future on the race issue?

It's hard to tell. One thing you can believe is that things will always get better. They must learn new associations, how to deal with people. When I came to Alexandria, in 1970, we lived in a mixed neighborhood in Parkfairfax, down near Valley Drive. It was less than a mile from my work. Then we moved to Colonel Ellis Avenue in Seminary Ridge.

Melvin Miller

Interviewed on April 13, 2006

Melvin Miller worked as a lawyer in the civil rights arena for years and participated in the second Brown decision of 1955. He is now retired and active in civic affairs. He currently chairs the Alexandria Redevelopment and Housing Authority.

Tell me about yourself. Where did you grow up and how did you get to Alexandria?

I grew up in Haddenfield, New Jersey, south of Philadelphia, in a very wealthy town; my family brought down the average income. I went to public elementary and high school in Haddenfield. Elementary school was quite important to me. There were a dozen or so of us African-Americans of school age. They sent us to a two-room school with two teachers—grades 1–4 and 5–7. At best there were maybe nineteen or twenty students in the seven grades. You learned a lot from hearing lessons in the grades above yours. Then I went to St. Augustine's College in Raleigh, North Carolina. One of the reasons I went there was that the tuition was sixty dollars a semester.

I was only sixteen when I started college. We regular college students were afraid of you World War II veterans—you got a check each month, and we had none. After leaving St. Augustine's, I went to law school at Howard, where I graduated in 1955. I intended to go to Richmond because one of my instructors said that was the place to go. During that period most civil rights activities were taking place at Howard. I worked on the second Brown case and all the arguments that were put together there. We students critiqued it. It was hard not to believe in civil rights. Then I passed the Virginia bar but got drafted and spent two years in the Army. The firm in Richmond that I was going to work for had split up by them.

My wife and I got married in Alexandria; it was the first time either of us had been here. My wife said, "Why don't you go there and hang out a shingle? If nothing works out, you can always go to work for the government." So in January 1958, I began general practice, whatever came my way. The civil rights movement was starting then. Housing for African-Americans was terrible. We roomed with a teacher who lived across from my office. Housing was very segregated then and there was none for African-Americans. I joined with Otto and Sam Tucker in a case. When sit-ins started, I represented sit-ins in Virginia, down through Fredericksburg.

When the law had to be complied with, what was the reception to desegregation of Alexandria schools? Was John Albohm the superintendent then?

Actually the desegregation order came before John Albohm—T.C. Williams was superintendent. He was very reluctant to desegregate. The first African-American students entered white schools here in 1959, five years after the Brown decision. During those years we had pupil placement in Virginia. We fought it in the courts. In 1964, Dr. Albohm decided to close Parker-Gray, the city's black high school. Neighborhoods were so segregated, so actually this put most of black high school students into George Washington, but T.C. opened about then as the third high school. Then we went through Parker-Gray becoming a middle school. That was part of the desegregation effort, but if you move people, you never solve it because of housing patterns.

Was there lots of heat?

Yes, when they created the 2-2-2 plan, making T.C. the city's only high school. Marshall Beverly, Don Baldwin, and others fought desegregation. My son was in the Cub Scout den where Baldwin's wife was the den mother. Things were very heated. Lots of good people supported desegregation, but by and large they were silent.

Even in our Afro-American leadership group there was some divergence. Marion Johnson and I became close enough through the city's Human Relations Council. Eileen Eddy was a leader of that group, which came to espouse the more liberal feelings. I on the other hand went along but I didn't think they were pushing enough. These changes take time, especially if you don't do anything. Quite frankly, an old group of folks controlled Alexandria at the time and they were dead set against desegregation.

Did some blacks like being separate?
That depends on who you talked to. The black community had some very good things. Resources were lousy, but we had good teachers who concerned themselves with kids. When my wife first came here to teach, they required every black school teacher to make a home visit to every child. That went away when we began to integrate. She taught at Lyles-Crouch. Some of her students lived in the projects. I drove her there and sat outside while she made home visits in the projects. The community was a part of the education of black kids.

What could have been done in a way that was more effective?
We did it in steps, always when pressure was applied. It didn't really come from the heart. I'd have asked where do we want to go and do it all at once. You can't ease your way into integration, people become accustomed to it. When Alexandria merged the high schools, people felt we could have done the elementary schools in a rational way and get over their angst.

But some scars are left after every battle. Think of the Supreme Court words: with all deliberate speed. What does this mean? We don't know yet.

Who do you remember as key people making it work or trying to make it work?

I was on the outside, but I can't help but think about the school boards—they don't get a lot of credit for making tough decisions—most were not close votes, and they were not the most popular. People like Ferdinand Day, Alison May, Bob Wood, Connie Ring, Tim Luckett (I figured he was the enemy because he was part of the old-boy network, but he took some strong stands). I look at people who were making decisions rather than those who didn't have a vote. I'd have loved to see them be more far-reaching with each decision, but when you sit on the board it's a different ball game.

Was John Albohm forceful or did he go where the wind was the strongest?

I always admired John Albohm. He was a master politician and I appreciated that. Many times I went to him with problems and would leave feeling I'd accomplished something, but then I asked myself what did I get? But he was the right person for the job at that time. I can't imagine anybody else pulling it off like he did. He kept the board together. He did what was needed in Alexandria at the time. This was never a vicious place, but the feelings were not perhaps as bad as they sounded. If we could get the law out of the way, people would get along.

Where is it going now? What do you see in the future for Alexandria public schools and diversity?

I will answer in a couple of ways. One has to be in the governance issue—with the school board. I oppose elected school boards. We're seeing the result of it now with the current election. When the school board members were appointed, we could count on Council picking good people to serve it.

The second issue is the economic issue, the housing issue. We're slowly getting to where the city is not able to maintain a lot of diversity. Only 11 percent of city employees, including teachers, live in the city. It is a struggle to maintain diversity, particularly within schools.

I'm one of the great advocates for Alexandria and its schools. I wouldn't live anywhere else. It's a good city and it has a good school system, though things need to be corrected. It is more subtle now.

Mickey Moore

Interviewed on May 3, 2006

Mickey Moore served in the Alexandria school system for 32 years, first as a social studies teacher, then as an administrator. She retired in 1988 as Assistant Superintendent.

Tell me where you were born, your background, and how you wound up in Alexandria.

I was born in Murray, Utah, in 1930. I went to Jordan High School and then to the University of Utah, where I majored in American history. Of course I also took the required education credits. I taught for three years in the Jordan School District, then spread my wings to come east when I got a job in the Alexandria schools. I spent 32 years in Alexandria City Public Schools, most of them at Hammond, a high school that had just opened in 1956. It was the first secondary school built in the city since George Washington High School was built in 1935. It was a big thing for Alexandria. The school was all white, which I was used to because we had no blacks in Jordan. The darkest kids we had there were Mexicans. There was no separate school for them, they sat with the white kids—and there were not a lot of them.

The first live black I ever saw was at the University of Utah, but he was a foreign exchange student, not an American black, so imagine my thoughts when I came to Alexandria. There was definitely more than one black in this city. I got my master's from American University in American history. My thesis was on the effect of the gold rush on the Mormon community in

Salt Lake City. It was an interesting topic. A former teacher, my 12th grade English teacher, suggested it. Dr. David Miller at the University of Utah said it was a good topic so I pursued it. Since I went home every summer to help my mother I could do research for my thesis at the Utah Historical Society in Salt Lake City.

How many were there in your family?
 Six lived to adulthood. That was typical out there. Kids were needed to help on the farm.

When you came to Alexandria, what was your sense of the reception to the Brown decision in 1954? You came in 1956.
 The subject was not a major concern at Hammond. It just wasn't discussed by faculty or students. Of more concern was the presidential election. T.C. Williams was the superintendent of schools. He was diametrically opposed to integration; he delayed it as long as he could. Finally he had no other course but to integrate a token number of blacks.

How about the community at large? How did people feel then?
 I didn't really hear much. I didn't live in Alexandria then. I think people felt that if you don't talk about it, it will go away. But Alexandria then, as now, was an educated community and far more liberal than you'd think for a Southern town.
 It was calm here, I never heard desegregation discussed. I can't remember. The black community was not demanding. Parker-Gray, the black high school, was a good school. The teachers were strict and competent. They did use corporal punishment and the parents backed them up. If it hadn't been such a good school, there could have been trouble. George Washington High School was recognized throughout the state. Hammond was known for its academic standards. If Parker-Gray hadn't had

the reputation as a good high school, this could have caused problems.

What about the Departmental Progressive Club?
As a teacher, I never heard of the Progressive Club. I don't know what went on behind closed doors. That idea in the movie, *Remember the Titans*, of whites acting up—that wasn't true. Whites didn't rock the bus. The same when Hammond integrated. Hammond was a high-class school; we had the reputation of being snobs. We had a good faculty. Teachers were not sloppy, they would have been ostracized by the staff. We maintained high standards. Our integration was so quiet and went so smoothly that we couldn't believe it. People were programmed to think that white kids would walk out of class, that they would riot. That first day of integration was a let-down to staff and students who expected some excitement.

Pasty Ragland, one of the black students who integrated Hammond, was in my government classes. The class members didn't put their arms around her but they weren't mean to her either. She became a favorite among her classmates. On Fridays we always had current events, and I'll never forget that one student used the word *nigger* in his presentation. You could have heard a pin drop in room 244. It was all a new cultural experience for me. I had never been to school with a black, but I came out of my chair like I was shot. I told the kid never to use that word again in my presence. No one was on Donnie's side, they were on my side. Other than this incident, I can't remember any time when my students were rude to these black students.

Who would you identify in the community and in the schools as key people to help with desegregation, make it easier to work?
One was Mrs. Mary Walton Livingston, Betsy's mother, and Gus King's father. She was a liberal community leader who

had a sense of justice. He was a magistrate or judge. With their friends, they fought to keep the schools in Virginia open during the days of massive resistance. In Prince Edward County, the schools closed and they established academies for white students only. A whole generation of black kids grew up there without any education. So I would say Mr. King and Mrs. Livingston were two influential leaders among whites. State Senator Armistead Boothe was another one. Marian Galland, Alexandria's Delegate to the General Assembly, was also active in keeping the schools open.

As far as the schools were concerned, we didn't get on the soap box. We went along with the superintendent. What you thought might be something else, but nobody would go against T.C. Williams. John Albohm, his successor, was from New York. He came here directly from a position in Pennsylvania, and he knew we had to do something. The courts were on us. It involved changing or being sued. That's the time I remember the most excitement from the community. The west end parents didn't like busing kids to G.W. They said no, we would lose our high school first. We lost a lot of fine patrons and students. They left the city; many went to Fairfax County. There was more acrimony over that than against integration. Busing and closing two successful high schools caused more unrest and problems than integration ever did.

The first black on the faculty at Hammond was Louis Johnson, a fine man and a good coach. We had a faculty dining area in the cafeteria and I remember when Coach Johnson came in. He tried to be as invisible as he could be but it was hard with a black face. He sat in the cafeteria with his sack lunch. I sat by him and introduced myself. The faculty accepted Coach Johnson, and the coaches adored him. Coach Johnson and I became good friends.

When I worked here from 1983–87, I knew the faculty at T.C. and in the schools were not overjoyed about desegregation.

That's absolutely correct. There were some dyed-in-the-wool gray people, "confederates." That goes back to their family history and also to the behavior of some black students. Change is always hard to accept and this change was especially hard.

During my first year of teaching here I was fascinated. It was a whole new world. I taught eighth graders, and they were so cute with their Southern accents. Most were 100 percent Southern. They argued about the Civil War. They took it seriously. It was the same with their families. They were strong confederates.

Were the Board members I knew—like Judy Feaver, Mary Jane Nugent, and Lou Cook—were they prominent in supporting desegregation?

I don't know.

Ruby Tucker has been around a long time, and Rosa Byrd. Ferdinand Day was always very gentlemanly. When would you say things became relatively smooth and the community accepted the fact that the majority was the minority and kids seemed to get along rather well?

There were no riots—a lot of the trouble was over drugs, not race. T.C. was my worst experience. The Hammond kids didn't want to be there, nor did the G.W. kids, and T.C. kids didn't want them there. At T.C. they went to their own groups, so did the faculty. We didn't want to leave Hammond, and some wept. G.W. teachers had a strong loyalty to that school. T.C. had not been open long enough for those teachers to develop loyalty. T.C. opened in 1965. T.C.'s success in sports helped them, but they could have had girl scouts on the team. You can't put three strong high schools together and expect not to win. The choice of the football coach caused a lot of feelings. Bill Yoast had every reason to become the coach but they put

Boone in because he was black and the superintendent was under pressure to appoint a black.

Was Boone portrayed accurately in Remember the Titans?
No, but that's another story. You can thank Ferdinand Day for Boone being there. A black could have been the basketball coach and leave Yoast as football coach. That would have stopped all that nonsense. Whites didn't like it, the kids didn't like it. Blacks, right or wrong, though they owned basketball. In Utah white boys can jump. That coaching decision really did not help the situation. White boys were told they weren't welcome in the locker rooms.

Here's my last question. This is your opportunity to say what you want to say about the subject. Where do you think Alexandria is headed?
I think the best days of the Alexandria school system are definitely over. The quality of teachers coming in now is no match for the quality that once was. The same could be said of administrators and students. We no longer demand that things be done right. A lot of mediocre teaching is going on but we can't fault the teachers because they have difficult kids to teach. The parents are to blame for some of it but some are working two jobs, so they're not home to look after the kids. The kids are free to roam. There's a breakdown in society generally, and this is not just in Alexandria. It's across America. I worry about America and its institutions, including public education.

John Porter

Interviewed on April 24, 2006

John Porter, a native Alexandrian, was principal of T.C. Williams High School for 22 years before moving to the central office in 2006 as Assistant Superintendent for Administrative Services and Public Relations.

Tell me where you grew up, how you got to where you are, and what it was like to grow up in Alexandria.

I was born in Washington, D.C., in 1947, but my family lived in Alexandria. I grew up on Rosemont Avenue by the train tracks. There were row houses there but now they are called town houses. I remember fondly the trains going by—steam engines then—and I've always been fond of trains. I like a fan or some background noise when I sleep. In those days the schools didn't have kindergarten except through the local churches. I attended the Del Ray Methodist Church kindergarten, then went to first grade at Maury, grades 1–6—that would have been in the early 1950s.

In seventh grade I went to Lee School because Maury was not large enough to include seventh grade, too. We were bused to Lee from Maury. Seventh grade was my bad year and I ended up in summer school. That's a difficult age. Academically I was not applying myself. It was not the teacher's fault. My younger son had the same teacher for math at G.W. years later, and things didn't work out well for him there either.

For eighth grade, students had two options. Hammond had opened so you could go there for grades 7–8. Students in this end went to Jefferson, the old Alexandria High School. It consisted of two old mammoth buildings on a twenty-foot hill back then. It had a track and tennis courts on the northeast corner behind it.

Then I went to George Washington High School for four years. I didn't excel academically but I had a good time, doing what I needed to do. My dad served in World War II. He was an auto body painter, he painted vehicles, starting at Herby's Ford, which is now Ourisman Ford, located where La Porta is now on Duke Street. Then my dad became an auto body man and ended up working for the government at Andrews Air Force Base. Mom dropped out of school to help her family and worked as a phone operator for forty-eight years. The one thing they told me was that I was going to college.

After high school I went to summer school to get a head start on college at North Carolina Wesleyan. My dad was from North Carolina and had often gone past the school. An uncle that I respected and an aunt were teachers. The brother-in-law of my dad's sister was head of the education department at North Carolina Wesleyan and a coach. I ended up there because of that family connection—he'd watch over me.

That summer I took English and something else. When I came back in the fall, I didn't know what I wanted to do. I began the required courses, and I ran for student office. I don't know what inspired me to do that. I became vice president of the freshman class, and Dana was president. The Vietnam War was in progress and the draft was heating up. It was a tough time for kids—we felt lots of pressure to stay in school and do well or go to the service. People asked, "Why aren't you in the service?"

You had to pass a test to keep your deferment. Some kids were going to school just for deferment. I passed the test. Midway through our freshman year, the class president didn't make the grade so I assumed the presidency of the freshman class. I also became president for the sophomore, junior, and senior class. I graduated with honors in history.

In high school, during my sophomore year of 1962–63, Alexandria began token desegregation. A teacher named Roger McKay was a student at Parker Gray when I went to George Washington. We didn't understand why we had two high schools. People had strong feelings about the beginning of the civil rights movement and about John Kennedy. Drugs were beginning to become a real issue then. They were not a big issue in high school, but alcohol was. I saw more alcohol usage in college, though it was a Methodist school. We didn't see much marijuana.

We had token desegregation at G.W., our high school. Five to seven black students came to G.W. as juniors. I remember a couple of kids by name. Nolan Dawkins, who is now a judge in town, was one of them. He was on the school's basketball team. That was in the early 60s.

I don't remember any of us as kids having any serious reaction to this. Some kids made fun of black kids, but I was not involved in that. For my high school years, that was the extent of desegregation from my perspective.

Recently the *Gazette-Packet* did a story about desegregation and I suggested talking to Nolan Dawkins. Certain families said they'd be pioneers, on the front line. Charlie Hill and Nolan formed a band and practiced at Charlie's house.

When I went off to college, I saw crosses burning, half a mile from the college. The South was still not willing to change. We had a few black students at my college. I'm not sure whether the college admitted a number of black students by choice or because they feared a lawsuit.

I came home in 1969 to teach, and felt lucky to get a job. A former teacher helped me get the job. Lots had happened with desegregation. The school system was segregated by neighborhood. In that first year I came back, I had a diversity of kids who were grouped by advanced, average, essential, then a low essential class, really below average. We had smaller class sizes at Parker-Gray Middle School.

We experienced a number of difficult years from the standpoint of all that was happening—the Vietnam War, the civil rights movement, and the King and Kennedy assassinations. There was a real outcry for civil rights. G.W. was set on fire, and we had to man the doors at Parker-Gray during our off periods to keep G.W. kids from causing problems at our school. I remember holding the door while a crowd outside was pushing on the door to get in.

At the same time a young man named Robin Gibson was killed at a 7-Eleven store on Commonwealth Avenue. A clerk shot and killed him over a pack of gum he thought he was stealing. That mirrored what was going on nationally and we were working through locally. I was at Parker-Gray for four years, and we faced many issues.

What was the atmosphere in the Alexandria community during those years all this action was taking place?

There were a variety of adult feelings—some entrenched in bigotry from their youth. However, Alexandria was one of those few communities that was very open and liberal minded in many ways.

Alexandria was misrepresented in the movie, *Remember the Titans*. There was resistance to desegregation before that time but it became more rare as time went on. In my fourth year at Parker-Gray I broke up a fight that was racially motivated. Mostly kids got into minor trouble, as kids do, but we had few fights. I was a crisis resource teacher to help kids solve problems and go back to class. Each year things got better, as a school and as a community.

In my fourth year at Parker-Gray I applied to become assistant principal at Hammond. In 1971–72, the Justice Department was threatening to sue the school system. John Albohm did a tremendous job getting us through this period in our history.

We decided on a 2-2-2 plan with T.C. as the city's only senior high school. Cross-town busing began. Elementary schools went to the K-3-3 model. Schools that were predominantly white were paired with schools predominantly black. Kids went to kindergarten in their own neighborhood school, then for three years went to that same school and were bused to the other paired school.

Parents complained about how many schools their kids had to go to. That was a valid point, and it did tear at the community a bit. Both our boys went to Lyles-Crouch for three years, out of our neighborhood.

We had some very supportive parents at T.C.—the Bigelows, Elliotts, Mulroneys—who stayed with schools. A number of people said we're going to make this work. They had a feeling of commitment to the larger cause. They said we don't want to sacrifice anything but we must stand firm for the bigger good of our city and country, and our kids will be better for it.

Rocky Mount Senior High School in North Carolina desegregated the year after I graduated from college. Private academies developed throughout the South. Rocky Mountain Senior High became majority minority. In Prince Edward County, Virginia, they closed the schools down rather than desegregate.

When I was a teacher I was not involved in the day-to-day operation of schools. A young man, Wendell Evans, was an active African-American, a voice for the kids. He lives in Maryland now, but he came over to a T.C. basketball game last year. From the kids' view, he was "a mover and a shaker." Fred Day, Melvin Miller. Hazel Rigby was an influential member of the teachers group. Teachers were dedicated to make it work. At Hammond in 1971, Jim Wilson and I went in as assistant principals. Jerry Hubbard was principal. We sat down before school began, and he said it's got to work this year. We had had so much upheaval during the last two years. It did work.

Bobby Howard was chair of the school board during that time, so he was caught in the middle of it. Alison May, another school board member a little later, was taking a lot of heat on both sides. Doug Harmon was city manager then. City officials, the school board and city council were all very supportive. Chuck Beatley was mayor then.

John Albohm, the superintendent, really carried us through—he was an outstanding politician. I introduced my wife to Dr. Albohm. When he offered me my first principal job at John Adams, I said, "Can I go talk with my wife about it?" and he said, "What's there to talk about? Oh yes, go ahead." He was a consummate politician, a central figure in working us through the issues of the time.

On the negative side—I encountered some bitterness in a number of staff members. Hammond people liked it as it was. I understand their feeling of commitment to staff, lots of feeling. Students at T.C. were upset (African-American students in particular) about the movie *Remember the Titans*. They're making too much of it, they said—it was our school. It was my football team and my school. It wasn't fair.

I remember some racial overtones and issues. In the west end of the city then, black families were sparse and many families were mobile. Some parents said they wouldn't send their kids to public schools, and more private schools sprang up.

My wife and I had a child in 1971 and one in 1976. In 1974, we decided to move from our condo in Fairfax. We moved back and bought a house on Myrtle Street because we wanted our kids to go to school here. It was a good investment in a number of ways.

"We'll cycle through these problems of integration. Now we have an immigration issue—Latinos are coming in large numbers. Our Alexandria schools were more diversified starting in the mid-1980s. We had a very small percentage of Asians, maybe 2–3 percent. The numbers of Middle East students was growing. We also had waves of immigrants from Vietnam, Cambodia, and Laos, then Ethiopia and El Salvador.

The media has helped over the years, though it focused much more on dramatic situations that led parents to worry about safety. We want the world to be perfect for our children, but sometimes it's better for kids to be protected. Ten or fifteen years ago, we started to hear that our kids who graduated from T.C. go off to college feel well prepared academically but they are also prepared to deal with the real world. They can move into a variety of groups, but their college classmates who come from upper middle class homogeneous schools don't know how to talk to students from other ethnic groups.

As we look back at major changes, it has been fascinating to be a part of it. I too wondered if we'd make it as a society and we did.

Roy Smith

Interviewed on July 21, 2006

Roy Smith is the former band director at two Alexandria high schools. He also played trumpet with various ensembles. He is now retired and living in Bellingham, Washington.

Roy, I'd like you to tell me where you grew up and how you wound up in Alexandria.

Well, I had lots of way stations along the way. I started out in Detroit. How did I get to Alexandria? My first stop was to Okinawa, the garden spot of the Pacific. When I came back I went to school in Cincinnati, and while I was there I got married. I thought I had a job teaching in Richmond, Virginia, at the Walter D. Moses Company but I ended up becoming an instrument salesman and they canned me because I told somebody that if the prices were too high for them at the Walter D. Moses Company, they should go down the block and around the corner and they might have some cheaper instruments. My manager heard me and canned me the next day.

So I was looking for a job and talked to somebody from the state department of education and he called me in December. I was selling remote control automobiles in Thalheimer's Department Store in Richmond. The gentleman's phone call led to an interview with T.C. Williams (Thomas Chambliss Williams), the superintendent, and his assistant, F.F. Brown (we called him foolish Frank Brown).

I sat on his bed in a hotel room. He was in a chair with Mr. Brown in another chair. All they were interested in was,

"Can you make the band march?" I had all these wonderful ideas in my head and had spent time in the service. I had studied music at the Cincinnati Conservatory of Music and had a master's under my belt.

"Well," they said, "can you make the high school band march?" I said, "I am sure I can. I think I can get them to do nearly anything you like, sir." I was a smart aleck then, still am. They said they'd call me back, and they did. I must have passed the interview because after meeting with T.C. Williams and Frank Bowen, I was hired.

I'm not sure when we met, probably later in the fall. I was to replace Phil Lester, a red-headed gentleman who was leaving teaching after Thanksgiving following the football season of 1952. They told me he had taught there ten years and the kids thought the sun rose and set on him, so I'd have a difficult position getting my program underway.

My salary was $3,200 a year, much better than the $2,800 I was offered in Louisiana where the last 100 yards I think I was expected to swing in by grapevine. I said, "I don't think I can do that." So I took T.C. up on his offer. That's how I got to Alexandria.

Roy, what do you recall the reaction was in Alexandria to the Brown decision and in the community and in the schools?

That decision didn't affect me that I remember. In 1957 the court order came. That's when I think Francis C. Hammond was integrated and three black kids came to us. Hammond began as a new school in 1956.

T. Marcus Gillespie was the principal at that time. We had meetings about how to get along with everybody. Sensitivity sessions, because we were going to be exposed to a whole new culture. I didn't have any problems with integration at that time at all. Sometimes those faculty meetings lasted forever. We had "time" pools going on and we placed small bets (one cent or two) to see how long they lasted. You could also submit a cartoon. The cartoon contest cost you a nickel. I don't remember who won the time pool, twelve or fifteen cents.

One of the entries in the cartoon contest was mine, and Jim Miller, a fantastic choral director at Hammond, submitted one. The rule was that the cartoon had to include things pertinent to that faculty meeting. Two subjects were: (1) we were to have three Negro children coming to our school, and (2) we needed a notary public because everyone in the school seemed to need a notary public and they didn't know where to find one. In my cartoon I had hundreds of heads in the auditorium with three little black heads and I said, "Man, look at all those colored kids!" I won twenty cents. Jim Miller's had a little black girl with blouse and skirt and she held a sign that said "Notary public $2." He should have won as far as I was concerned. That's the way I felt about it.

When the first day arrived and the three black kids were coming in, there were television cameras across the street. The press was there. When I drove by the school, I thought, "Good grief! What's going on?" There was no problem at the beginning when the kids came in. They weren't in the music program so I don't know really how that affected them.

How about people in the community? Not school people.

Some of the school staff thought that was the beginning of the end. I didn't have that feeling at all, coming from Detroit. I went to an integrated high school, so it was not a problem, even with athletic events. Not with me, anyhow. But some staff members said, "We're in for real trouble. You've never had to work with them." I said, "I went to school with them." I knew there was some animosity there to begin with.

Did you ever discuss integration with T.C. Williams?

No, there was no occasion for that.

When Albohm came and he had to respond to that court order and said you were in trouble, what was your reaction and staff reaction to Albohm?

I didn't have a problem with John Albohm. I don't remember any problem. Probably the usual things, maybe the same things you ran into, personality conflicts, but I got along with him all right. I don't remember John Albohm ever saying we were in trouble. Not about integration, anyhow.

I wish I had known him. I've heard some funny stories. I read Mark Howard's dissertation, it's a good dissertation. So somebody came up with a 6-2-2-2 plan.

It was received by the faculty as a "6-2-2-screw-you plan." We thought that plan was not going to work. I don't think it stayed around too long. When was that? Right around the time that T.C. won the state football championship. The damage for G.W. and Hammond was we became part of the two, the middle two, so T.C. Williams got the two upper grades, 11 and 12. Those of us at the middle schools were trying to deal with the ninth and tenth grades. It was not a popular decision. Also, Parker-Gray and Minnie Howard seventh- and eighth-grade schools were affected.

When T.C. opened up, I went from being a high school band director to a middle school band director. Actually it was definitely more fun being a high school band director.

One thing that resulted from the 6-2-2-2 plan was it made T.C. an athletic powerhouse and they won the state football championship. That was quite a feat. The coach at Hammond became the assistant coach. How did all that go down?

Not too well. Joe Adgate was the music and art curriculum specialist at the time. Joe knew I'd not be wild about having a middle school band when I'd had a topnotch high school band. As far as T.C. winning the state championship in 1971, they

217

had the best athletes from the three high schools that were in existence when they decided to go 6-2-2-2.

First of all, the Fairfax County schools objected quite a bit because T.C. would have a strong team. Not only did T.C. have one or two coaches—they had about six coaches—the G.W. coaches, and Hammond had Bill Yoast and an assistant, then the coach at T.C. Herman Boone was hired to be the head coach at T.C. They had all the coaches and all the football players they needed so they *should* have won the championship.

The sour grapes side is I was given the title of marching band director. That was a carrot, because Joe Adgate knew I was going to be a little bit upset. I knew I'd lose the high school band, though. Jack Dahlinger and I got along real well. It didn't really bother me that much after a while. But just like the football team, being in charge of the marching band, I had the best musicians from three high schools.

A little-known fact is that we won the state championship, too. When I shared the word that a movie was coming out *Remember the Titans*—with my good friend George Randall, he said that the name of the sequel would be *Remember the Band*! But we haven't gotten around to that yet.

Did you know Herman Boone?
Bill Yoast was a much easier man to deal with and work with.

Roy, do you recall how did the community of Alexandria, the citizens and the school board of Alexandria react to the desegregation plan?
The biggest complaint I heard was about the busing problem—that was a big problem. As far as the movie was concerned, they made it look like Alexandria was a redneck town, and I never had that feeling. Bill Yoast didn't live on a farm, either.

Did anybody play a significant role in helping it go through?

During the first week there was a major incident at Hammond. A group of white kids were chasing a black group, and as they came around the building it looked like the black group was chasing the white group. It kept going. When it was time for the buses, the white kids were across the street in an apartment project hiding behind a wall, and they threw rocks at the buses the black students were getting on. The black kids (I don't blame them) got off the bus and started chasing the white kids through the complex. Dick Hills and Ray Sanger were out there trying to help. I remember both Hills and Sanger standing out in the street, trying to get them to stop throwing rocks.

Alison May must have played a role.

If she did, I don't know that part of it. Ferdinand Day and other members of the school board tried to do something. The faculty couldn't do anything. Ray Sanger couldn't stop it, Dick Hills couldn't stop it, and the faculty couldn't do it. All we were doing that first or second day was dodging rocks.

That was quite different from what happened in Boston. The mind set a lot of people have is that Boston was outrageous in its reaction, but only one person was killed in Boston and Mayor Kevin White said Boston was scared to death. It was all fear that caused the problems. I can understand that because they paired the very poor South Boston with Roxbury, all black, coming in. It was the stupidest plan that Judge Garrity came up with.

There's a courtyard at Hammond and students would run from the front to the back. You didn't know who was after who. David Lloyd, one of the assistant principals, was in the courtyard trying to calm the kids when a white girl asked him who he was. He told her his name and said he was an assistant principal, and she said, "Oh, nobody likes you," and she ran off. David liked to tell that story.

John Porter and Jim Wilson were associate principals, too. On the other side of the coin, do you know of anybody who was active in trying to prevent desegregation, anybody who tried to stir up trouble?

Nothing I know about. I know the whole situation was bothering my family. At one point, my wife Alice said, "We don't see the fun side of you any more. All you do is come home and tell us all these bad things that are going on." I said, "Well, these things *are* going on. They *are* bad things." She was right, though, and I should have tried to keep more of the bad stuff to myself.

That's very understandable. Your insights are very valuable.

I was out of the loop in some areas. You should have asked me yesterday and then I could have thought about it. There's still racial bias in this country and that's a shame. I believe I have to go along with Bill Cosby in many ways because I think blacks have made a lot of contributions to help make this integration work—and in many ways white people have held onto their philosophies and their backgrounds and they don't want it to work. But unless they do, it's a question of power. I agree I'd like to see more black people tell it like they see it. I agree with Bill Cosby that the black people have to get out and do something, take credit or take the blame for some of the things that are going on now. The white folks should do the same.

I was surprised when I first got here that the schools were still segregated. Integration here not having been accomplished before. So far I think things have gone well. You can't look at the football point of view as being a success story for integration though it did happen for that team and for the band.

We had gone to band camps together prior to integration, when G.W. was basically a black school. At Parker-Gray, Cortelyou Payne was always given the job of taking care of the black students. Art Dawkins was another one. We had our merry band of whites, but we never had any racial disturbances at band camps either. Even when we integrated, I don't recall any racial tension within the bands.

Music has been integrated for many many years—jazz. That's when I first got acquainted with integration, nobody cared as long as you could blow, you had the feeling. A lot of people play technically but don't have any soul. It's technique!

Epilogue

"A racist system inevitably destroys and damages human beings; it brutalizes and dehumanizes them, black and white." This statement by Kenneth Clark was included in the *New York Times* obituary of the educator on May 2, 2005.

In a *New York Times* interview with Clark in 1973, he said, "One of the things that disturbs me most is the sophisticated form of intellectual white backlash."

Referring to Daniel Patrick Moynihan and others, Clark said, "In their ivory towers, they have lost all empathy with low-income people and black people. They are seeking to repudiate their own past liberal positions, fighting against their own heritage at the expense of the poor."

Clark's disillusionment was deep, and he felt he had failed. In 1992 he said, "I am pessimistic, and I don't like that. I don't like the fact that I am more pessimistic now than I was two decades ago."

I disagree with Kenneth Clark, although his disillusionment is understandable. Surely, desegregation improved the achievement of poor black students. Moving from schools with calculated limited and antiquated resources, including many ill-prepared and incompetent teachers, helped kids fortunate enough to be bused to schools with better teachers and greater resources.

What kind of society would exist today without the effort to desegregate schools? Allowing neighborhoods to remain as they were with *de facto* and *de jure* black and white populations could easily divide a segregated America even more, and certainly delay any semblance of an integrated society. Perhaps, over time, and with new generations of Asian and Hispanic populations, the public schools would reflect diversity naturally with no busing required.

By moving children to different neighborhoods, more children gained some awareness of each other's culture. Some ugly confrontations were inevitable. One reason for the remarkable growth of the black middle class can be attributed to desegregated schools. Granted, the percentage of black students in advanced placement or International Baccalaureate programs was extremely low; the idea of a better life and more opportunities was planted in many black youths. Formerly, in their neglected and inferior segregated schools, they saw little opportunity to upgrade their lives.

The language of the Supreme Court and stated in Chief Justice Earl Warren's opinion made clear the devastating impact of black children made to feel inferior.

Has the feeling of inferiority diminished? I believe so, but much of it remains as incidents occur daily that imply the continued sense of still being, if not inferior, then certainly of feeling like an outsider. The Black Power movement of the 1960s and the growth of Black Muslims play roles in dealing with this issue.

There is little doubt that the power of expectations of teachers toward black children has improved. This is reflected in classrooms and communities. Progress has been made and the recognition of the importance of expectations in evident.

The insights that Gunnar Myrdal expressed in his book, *An American Dilemma*, ring true today. He wrote that race is a major, if not *the* social problem in America. Yet undeniable gains have been made. The history covering the struggles of desegregation establishes in my mind the value of the effort.

Was desegregating public schools successful? What have I learned from my experiences as a teacher and superintendent? Can the slice of history I experienced from the 1960s, 1970s, and 1980s contribute to a clearer understanding of how to accomplish change? Did desegregation change social mores?

These and many other questions can be raised regarding the attempts to desegregate America's public schools. My experience evolved from naïve idealism driven by a passion to correct past injustices to a pragmatic approach, still highly motivated, to steadily lessen the gap between upper- and middle-class kids and the ever-growing numbers of children of poverty.

Having the advantage of loving parents is enormous. Just being read to, plus the varying ways of stimulating interest in books, in nature, and in what is happening in the world at all levels makes a difference that is inevitably revealed in schools.

The old adage of learning the hard way, examining past mistakes, and building upon lessons learned paves the way to smoother and more successful experiences.

Obviously, individual assessments of desegregation differ widely and depend upon an individual's circumstances. Telling comments from individuals actively involved in four cities where I worked reveal the complexities of desegregation. Reverend Lewis Powell comments:

> The problem of the Jefferson County School System continues to be the lack of black teachers hired by the system. Before desegregation, the Louisville system had more than 1,000 black teachers. Upon desegregation and merger, the black teachers were phased out and literally pushed out of the system. But the system has never regrouped and regained these teachers for several reasons—lack of an aggressive recruiting team, teachers within the system who felt the system was not salable, and lack of aggressiveness by staff members who have been given the charge to recruit. At this date the system has an 800 black teachers gap. A total of 853 black teachers are in the system today.

Students interviewed were overwhelmingly positive in their reactions.

A white sophomore at Western High School in Louisville said, "We learn from each other. I like the mix."

An African-American senior at Ballard High School said, "Blacks get in trouble both ways. We are called Oreos, academic snobs, or hostile by other students, black or white."

A white senior at Ballard said, "I have lived such a sheltered life, coming from a private school and all-white neighborhood. It's great to be in a mixed school."

My interviews with high school students in focus groups, talking with them individually, and observing them in schools confirm the above statements. School reputation and program choice are more important to secondary students.

With the vision of hindsight, supporters of desegregation underestimated the degree of emotion that erupted in districts affected by the court's rulings. Admittedly, there was an arrogance, unintended though it may have been, that accompanied efforts to desegregate schools.

Conversing with Moe Coleman in Pittsburgh reminded me of my attitude during those years. Moe told me:

> Maybe school desegregation hastened suburbanization in the country. But the GI Bill, the ability to get cheap housing, the interstate highway, all played a role. Running away from racial tension was a factor, but not the only one. In looking back, I think I and others were denigrating to the white working class. We called them rednecks, but they were trying to hang onto their limited resources. You can understand why they disliked intellectuals commenting on issues affecting their families. Sure, there were racists among these ethnic groups.

The loss of white middle class kids happened in all metropolitan areas, including Pittsburgh, Boston, Louisville, and Alexandria, where I was involved as an educator. Surely there are impressive examples of success. Equally certain are disappointing, even tragic, stories.

What are the lessons learned? The Pittsburgh story is intriguing. From the 1960s to the mid 1990s, an evolution from the concept of the Great High School to magnet schools and a feeder system to achieve a reasonable degree of integration shows recognition of why a high school of 5,000 teenagers is next to impossible to succeed. The costs of providing the staffing necessary to provide individual achievement is enormous. Add the need to maintain a stable, trained team-teaching approach is difficult. With the constant change of board members, along with periods of political partisanship tied to an ideology, only an authoritarian government could manage.

Dealing directly and honestly with communities in their neighborhoods is a lesson that is verified by current times. This lesson is much easier to describe than to actually carry out.

Social engineering reminds us of Franklin D. Roosevelt's New Deal. Social engineering is a pejorative charge aimed at an idea like busing children out of their neighborhoods. Yet isn't there evidence of social mores linked to racial separation a form of an apartheid system? Do we not live in an age where overt discrimination in housing, language, and everyday living demonstrates that over time mores do indeed change? Joseph Ellis's study of George Washington, *His Excellency*,[1] uses in his words "the privileged perspective of the present."

Boston's experience has a clear lesson. Do not bus children to neighborhoods that have developed racial prejudice and hatred for decades. Recall Judge Garrity responding to my question:

> What would I do differently if I think about it? Well, for one thing, I would try much harder to work closely with local officials, especially during the early stages of the process. Although our positions were upheld by the courts, being "always right" and they being "always wrong" created a distrusted atmosphere, when collaborative problem solving might have led to some solutions.

> Another mistake we made was not to work more closely with parents. We just assumed that they would eventually overcome their prejudices and send their kids to the school we selected to serve the common good. How arrogant!

Louisville/Jefferson County presents a promising example. Again, there are lessons to be learned. Different from Boston and its innumerable towns and cities with their own independent jurisdictions, Louisville/Jefferson County had advantages for desegregation. Moreoever, the Kentucky Education Reform Act (KERA) mandates that school-based councils make their own budget decisions. Now, at least, decision making involves more parents, teachers, and school-based staff. The days of central administration and its bureaucracy making decisions and regulating how the schools carry out orders from central headquarters are fading rapidly. Moreover, the superintendent, Stephen Daeschner, who succeeded Donald Ingwerson in 1992, is still leading the system.

It is understandable, especially in today's atmosphere, filled with anxiety over the safety of their children, why parents are motivated to have neighborhood schools—ideally within walking distance. When you add the intensity of the African-American community insisting on neighborhood schools for their children, you realize that advocates for desegregation must adopt alternative approaches.

In reality, there are some locations or areas where the chances for accomplishing desegregation are greater than those in more hostile environments. Certainly, a comprehensive plan is necessary and must be rigorously supported. Richard Wallace's twelve-year tenure as superintendent—from 1980 to 1992—demonstrates that total effort is a must. Recall Wallace's comments in the Pittsburgh sections:

For the first three or four years, I had to negotiate with the Human Relations Commission as we tried to integrate the elementary schools and the high schools. And we did it again through magnet programs. I convinced them that if we were to create special programs, we were able to integrate schools voluntarily. For example, we made South High School a high-quality vocational school, working closely with area businesses. At Schenley High School, which was 87 percent black, we established a teacher center in 1981. When we started there, it was the lowest achieving secondary school and it is now the second ranking school in the city. For ten years it has been 50 percent racially balanced.

Interestingly, the fellow who became Board President, an African-American and strong advocate for desegregation, had been a "doubting Thomas" in the early 1980s. I remember how he testified before the Human Relations Commission and said our plan would not work. Three years later, when we went to testify again in Philadelphia, a fellow Board member reminded him of how he was opposed to our plan, including the magnet program at Schenley High School, where his children went. Jake, now the Board president, replied, "I was wrong. It *is* working!" He became the strongest supporter of the plan, and rallied the black community behind it. In five years, the achievement of black children nearly doubled, over 60 percent of the national norms.

In Phase Two of our school improvement plan, we trained principals and matched administrative interns for two years with principals of high-achieving black schools. Several of these interns became successful principals using techniques learned during their internships.

Obviously, it is essential for wide-scale generous funding combining private and public funding. By concentrating on community development, the Ford Foundation and the Mott Foundation are providing significant funding to build support for schools that are open seven days a week and operate day and night. Young adults and students combine their studies with those needs in poor areas that are struggling to survive.

The earliest example of this sort of community school was established and continually embellished by Leonard Covello, principal of Benjamin Franklin High School in East Harlem from 1934 to 1956.[2] Such a concept was non-existent back in the 1930s. Not so today, as the community school approach is attracting attention throughout the country. Covello was not thinking about desegregation when he was developing an ever-expanding concept of how a school can be the center for bringing young people and adults together. Indeed, the power being shared with the citizens of East Harlem made the school the unifying force. The concept of the community school has clear implications for integrating a community. It requires focus, adjustments, and consistent attention for success to be achieved.

What does the story of desegregation mean for the future? The uniqueness of the human specie makes it impossible to predict. I ponder my lifelong experience with race—the joy of success, the agony of disappointment, and the frustration of overwhelming complexity. And my answer is: Keep on trying, be not afraid to learn, even if the new knowledge contradicts what was once believed.

Notes

1. Joseph Ellis, *His Excellency*, Knopf Publishing Group, 2004, p. 110.
2. Robert W. Peebles, *Leonard Covello*, Arno Press, 1967.